PRAISE FOR *ALL MY FRIE...*

"Need some friends but don't know how to make them? Amanda shares how to choose them. Need to shed some unhealthy relationships? Amanda details how to let them go. Need to be a better friend? Amanda models how to safely and smartly risk for connection. In *All My Friends Have Issues*, Amanda Anderson becomes the friend we've always needed and, in the process, helps us become a better friend so we can make better friends. At last! No more nose pressed against the glass, looking in from the outside. The door is open! Come on in, grab a spot on the couch, and dive in."

—Elisa Morgan, president emerita of MOPS International, cohost of *Discover the Word*, speaker, and author of *The Prayer Coin*, *The Beauty of Broken*, and *Hello, Beauty Full*

"Amanda Anderson describes the emotional and psychological foundations of healthy friendships in this captivating and often hilarious book. Offering her own experiences with warm vulnerability, she's written an entertaining and informative book!"

—Milan and Kay Yerkovich, authors of *How We Love* and *How We Love Our Kids*

"Be ready to laugh and then to learn as Amanda shares her weaknesses and foibles in her relationships with herself and her friends. But it's more than a laughing matter, for in the midst of her vulnerability she makes powerful points about what it takes to be an authentic friend. You will be a better friend from reading this book."

—David Stoop, PhD, clinical psychologist and author of *You Are What You Think* and *Change Your Thoughts, Change Your Life*

"*All My Friends Have Issues* is a fresh and current look at an important subject—female friendships. Amanda takes the reader on the journey of developing authentic friendships that will encourage, sharpen, and lead us to a place of rich connections with other women. This book is fun and informative. After years of working with women, this is a book I would highly recommend!"

—Debbie Alsdorf, speaker and author of *It's Momplicated* and *The Faith Dare*

"God never intended for us to go through life alone. And though we know this truth, we find ourselves alive during an interesting time in history. Social media enables us to be 'friends' with people we've never actually met. Connected 24-7 via the internet, studies have shown people are more lonely and isolated than ever before. In many ways we have lost the art and skill of making friends and being a good friend. In *All My Friends Have Issues*, Amanda guides us with thoughtful steps of how to form and maintain healthy friendships with actual people in real time. Written with personal examples, principles from Scripture, and relatable topics, this book is needed and necessary. Highly practical and enjoyable to read, Amanda's style is warm, funny, authentic, and relatable."

—Vivian Mabuni, speaker and author of *Open Hands, Willing Heart: Discover the Joy of Saying Yes to God*

ALL MY
friends
HAVE
ISSUES

ALL MY friends HAVE ISSUES

Building Remarkable Relationships
with Imperfect People (Like Me)

AMANDA ANDERSON

NELSON
BOOKS

An Imprint of Thomas Nelson

Published in Nashville, Tennessee, by Nelson Books, an imprint of Thomas Nelson. Nelson Books and Thomas Nelson are registered trademarks of HarperCollins Christian Publishing, Inc.

Published in association with the literary agency of WordServe Literary Group, Ltd., www. wordserveliterary.com.

Thomas Nelson titles may be purchased in bulk for educational, business, fund-raising, or sales promotional use. For information, please email SpecialMarkets@ThomasNelson.com.

ISBN 978-1-4002-0858-6 (eBook)
ISBN 978-1-4002-0857-9 (TP)

Library of Congress Control Number: 2019938089

Printed in the United States of America

19 20 21 22 23 LSC 10 9 8 7 6 5 4 3 2 1

For my J's:
Especially Jen, Josie, and Gina.
Thank you for loving me so well, issues and all.

And for Sophia and Olivia:
May you always find, as your mama has,
friends that point you to Jesus.

Most of all, love each other as if your life depended on it. Love makes up for practically anything.

—1 PETER 4:8 THE MESSAGE

Turk and I met over a Bloomin' Onion. I like to think of it as a metaphor for our relationship because it's delicious, but not really so healthy.

—J. D. IN SCRUBS

CONTENTS

PART 1: AUTHENTICITY

PART 2: ENCOURAGEMENT

CONTENTS

INTRODUCTION

A Real Friend

"Marilla," she demanded presently, "Do you think that I shall ever have a bosom friend in Avonlea?"

"A—a what kind of friend?"

"A bosom friend—an intimate friend, you know—a really kindred spirit to whom I can confide my innermost soul. I've dreamed of meeting her all my life."

—L. M. MONTGOMERY, *ANNE OF GREEN GABLES*

I was about seven years old when I began to feel the deep need for a good friend. Not having a car, I started making friendships of convenience. Next door there was a girl about my age who possessed an incredible collection of Barbie dolls, which I was forbidden to own, so she held instant allure. She and I never really shared a soul connection, however, and one day when she burned me with a cookie sheet and didn't really apologize, I'm afraid I lost interest. As my friend Terry is now fond of saying, that told me everything I needed to know.

Fortunately, down the street, I found my first *real* authentic, encouraging friend. When I first saw Vicki, we were in the fourth grade and she was sitting on her Stingray bicycle in front of her house. She had auburn hair and a lot of freckles and seemed like a slightly dangerous Anne of Green Gables. We became friends and remained close through high school. We attended each other's celebrations, school plays, and soccer games; comforted each other through breakups (with high school boyfriends and between her parents); and held each other to a high standard. Vicki could spot me being "fake" from across the quad and would later call me on it. Because I had two younger brothers and no sisters, the constancy of Vicki's friendship met my deep need for sisterhood.

In our early twenties, we were maid of honor in each other's weddings and we still keep in touch though we live two states apart. As I look back on our loving, life-affirming, super-fun friendship, Vicki and I were lucky enough to have found at age nine what many grown women still yearn for.

Vicki was—and is—pretty weird, but her weirdness was compatible with mine. We were both an odd combination of wacky child and teenage, boy-crazy bookworm. We could go for almost a whole afternoon speaking to each other using only movie dialogue or inside jokes (*Ferris Bueller's Day Off* and *The Princess Bride* were favorites), and anytime we put our name on a waiting list (for bowling, for a booth at Denny's) we said it was Ezmerelda. We thought we were hilarious even if no one else did. She confirmed we were kindred spirits when on our first day of high school English, she turned to the girls sitting next to us and said, "Hi, I'm Vicki. Want to be my friend?"

Of course, our friendship wasn't perfect. We also had regular conflicts, but those strengthened our friendship. Through them, we learned how to care for each other better in the future and built trust that we would give and receive forgiveness. To this day, I see this as a mark of a remarkable friendship: conflict makes it stronger rather than more precarious.

And that's where my friendship story gets a little more complicated.

Throughout my adolescence and early adulthood, another type of friendship ran in a parallel track: one that was filled with drama and strife. For years, those friendships would absorb a huge percentage of my spiritual and emotional energy, but I also lived in constant fear of losing them. Arguments made me feel like I was walking on eggshells, and I would wonder, *Whose issues are worse? Mine or theirs?* I became paranoid of displeasing these friends and was hyper-focused on securing my place in their lives. An undercurrent of competition and comparison flowed through those friendships, so I struggled to celebrate their victories—new friends, new jobs, new houses—because I feared they would cause my friends to surpass and outgrow me. I felt the reverse was true as well, that these girls/women weren't necessarily thrilled when I succeeded, because it made them feel small and insecure. Eventually, the relationship would end, not in a healthy or gradual way as when two friends grow apart because of geographic distance, but in a blowup that left one or both of us heartbroken.

I'd like to say I outgrew this pattern when I became a full-fledged adult, but I didn't. Even into my thirties, these two tracks continued to run: decades-long friendships that felt secure and fun-filled, and at least one friendship that felt uneasy and "off." Sadly, the squeaky friendship got the grease while the healthy ones got less of my attention.

Finally, I began to recognize certain similar issues in these relationships and had a harsh realization: I was the common denominator. So I entered a season of deep soul searching, prayer,

Bible reading, psychological research, and personal counseling. I read a lot about what it meant to have healthy boundaries, how to love people well, and what my own personal obstacles were. I even joined a twelve-step support group for Codependents Anonymous, in which "the only requirement for membership is a desire for healthy and loving relationships." In that program, reading through the *Codependents Anonymous Handbook* and swapping experiences with other women in the program, I learned some not-so-pretty truths about myself: issues of control, manipulation, dishonesty, and insecurity. But through "working the steps" I also began to get healthier and my perspectives began to recalibrate.

Eventually, I developed the discernment to spend energy in friendships that thrive—some I already had and new ones as well. And it didn't take finding perfect women without issues or becoming one myself. My friendships today are with imperfect women like me who have enough self-awareness that they can both give and receive the most important thing in any relationship: grace.

My favorite proverb about friendship is not from the Bible. It's an old Czech saying: "Do not protect yourself by a fence, but rather by your friends."

In high school, Vicki and I protected each other from bullies, brothers, and bad rumors. As adults, my friends and I still need relationships that are soft places to land, because we face new challenges: financial issues, trouble in marriages or dating relationships, strained family relationships, irascible bosses, willful kids, serious illnesses, and all manner of other hardships. I love the picture the Czech proverb paints of surrounding ourselves in a loving community, a place where we can let down our guard, find peace, and work out life with others.

Today, I'm proud of my community of women. To me, being safe in my friendships means sharing my thoughts, flaws, fears, sins, joy, and raw emotions and receiving love and acceptance rather than judgment, competition, and withdrawal in return. Safety is knowing that I will receive forgiveness when I repent and ask for it, and that my friends will apologize to me when I share how I've been hurt. It means that my confidences will be kept and God's good will for me encouraged. Because I'm sure of their affection and appreciation of me as a person, I find peace and comfort in my friends' wise counsel, even when they need to correct me.

The quality of our friendships is one of the determining factors in the satisfaction we feel in our lives. As C. S. Lewis wrote, "Friendship is unnecessary, like philosophy, like art, like the universe itself. . . . It has no survival value; rather it is one of those things which give value to survival."[1] The goal of this book is to define what healthy, safe friendships look like, how to cultivate them, and how to nurture the friendships you already have so that you can experience more fun, meaningful connection, and spiritual growth. I believe these benefits grow out of three foundations: *authenticity, encouragement,* and *accountability.*

> **Authenticity** allows us to reveal our true selves—both strengths and weaknesses—and be loved just as we are.
> **Encouragement** means celebrating each other's joys, comforting each other in sorrow, and spurring each other on to bravely be the best version of ourselves.
> **Accountability** reminds us of who we are and what we stand for—and it calls us out when we forget.

Beware: as you read, you may feel convicted to step out of some of your current relationships, or to shift a friend who has been on the inside circle of your life to a place a little farther from your heart. My hope, though, is that this book will help you grow in discernment, so you can determine if your friends' issues can be covered with grace or if you should take a step back from the relationship. You may also be convicted of some of your own unhealthy patterns as I have been, but I will give you some tools that I have found helpful in correcting them. (You can explore these ideas deeper on your own or in community by using the Reader's Guide at the end of the book.)

Throughout, I tell stories about my friends and me—issues and all—and I have not changed their names. Oddly, my closest friends over the last ten years are named Jen, Gina, Josie, Jodi, Jana, Jenny, and Jill; don't worry about trying to remember which *J* is which. You'll also hear about Sophie, Kelly, Wendy, and Elizabeth, and more about Vicki, who is still in my life.

These courageous women have given me their blessing to share their stories and struggles. We're modeling authenticity here, sisters, so that you may be inspired to go and do likewise: risk the time and vulnerability it takes to have remarkable friendships that encourage you in your life's purpose, hold you accountable to a high standard of integrity, and won't let you give up on the dreams of your heart.

As it turns out, I actually have a lot of healthy, safe friends today, and I'm still a little surprised by it. One theory on how this happened is that I need a lot of women so I can spread my high-maintenance issues around. My favorite theory, however, is that God blessed me with these awesome people because he knew I would write this book and needed the research. I'm grateful. To him. To them. For you, reader. So, join us. Let's take this risk together.

Part 1

AUTHENTICITY

We can choose to be perfect and admired or to be real and loved.

—GLENNON DOYLE MELTON, *LOVE WARRIOR*

Behold, you delight in truth in the inward being, and you teach me wisdom in the secret heart.

—PSALM 51:6 ESV

Chapter 1

CALLS FROM THE BATHROOM

Building an Authentic Foundation

Ross: What is Monica's biggest pet peeve?
Chandler: Animals dressed as humans!
Ross: That's correct.

—FROM *FRIENDS*, "THE ONE WITH THE EMBRYOS"

Bathrooms, though unhygienic and accident-likely places to use one's phone, are often where I make and receive important, authentic communications. This may hearken back to school days, when the girls' bathroom was a refuge. In the sixth grade, for example, I ran to the girls' room with Vicki after my boyfriend Peter broke up with me in front of the entire school. Vicki and I stood on the smelly ceramic tile, and she offered me this encouragement: forget Peter; she'd just go ask another guy to be my boyfriend. I, of course, consented. It might not have been the best advice, but it was certainly well-meaning and made a lot of sense at age twelve.

In my early twenties, one of my best friends, Kelly, called me from a bathroom while her fiancé was just outside the door. Weeks away from their wedding, her betrothed had made a confession about something in his past that threw her for an absolute loop. She questioned whether she should still marry him. I was heartsick for her. But also, I *knew* her, and I *knew* this guy. She and I had been roommates our senior year in college, and I had witnessed their courtship firsthand. I was pretty sure all signs pointed to forgiving him and forging ahead with the wedding. So I talked her out of that bathroom. I'm happy to say they've been married for eighteen years and he's one of the best husbands I know. (Phew.)

In my thirties and now in my forties, I've found that some of my best ways of coping with crisis, from family distress at Thanksgiving to a major frustration at work, is to hide in the bathroom and fire off a text to a close friend. I love both sides of my extended family dearly, but sometimes a skirmish about marshmallows on the sweet potatoes sends me running to a toilet seat where I can sit down and send a text message to someone who loves me enough to tell me I'm overreacting and need to calm down. I do find it a little embarrassing that I can't get through a holiday without some outside support, but I'm still a little uptight. I'm aware, and I'm working on it.

I confess I was checking my email in a Home Goods bathroom when the message came from my agent that this book was to be published. Without leaving the stall, I immediately called my husband followed by my friend Gina. It's official: you can know that I really love and trust you if I can't wait to exit the bathroom before I call you with good news.

But there have been times when my penchant for bathroom communications went horribly wrong.

Once upon a time, a good friend of mine was going through a bad divorce, the kind that originated in a systematic betrayal that leaves the wife feeling not just mad at her man, but convinced that men in general are no gosh darn good. I, not having particularly good boundaries at this stage in my life, set out to prove to her that there were still some great men in the world.

Specifically, there was one man I had met, a single father of a girl on my eldest daughter's soccer team, who was polite, funny, and had custody of his two adorable kids, which meant he'd convinced a court he was a great dad. So far, so good. He was also tall and nice looking—and totally bald. In our private conversations, we nicknamed him "Baldy but Goodie." We aren't proud of it, but it amused us and cheered my friend.

I told myself that I had no real intention of setting the two of them up; my friend's divorce wasn't even final yet. But then Goodie invited my family to his house for dinner.

On that rainy Sunday, the Academy Awards were on television, and I had a migraine, but we went. My husband Jeff, my kids, and I had a very nice time, and Jeff didn't notice that I was telling fewer stories than usual and asking more questions. We did talk about my husband's belief that there are several professions for which I would be ill-suited, one being an accountant and the other an international spy. Little did Jeff know that I was already on a secret spy mission.

Midway through the evening, I snuck my phone into the bathroom. I sent my friend a text that went something like this:

> House is immaculate. He cooked dinner. Work: manager at [company name here]. Divorced for 8 years, 80% custody of the kids. Disney Channel on, kids from the neighborhood all gather here. Cuts his son's meat. No mention of Jesus yet. My ringer is off. Text with additional questions.

I went back out to dinner and wondered why I had not received a response from my friend. After dinner, we said our goodbyes and before we'd pulled out of the driveway, I received a text from Goodie.

I think you meant to send this to someone else.

Oh. My. Gosh. I had sent this nice man a singles-ad style description of himself while a guest at his table! I went back and reread the text I had sent. *No mention of Jesus yet.* I groaned inwardly. I immediately texted off an apology and added, "Did I mention I have a single friend?" He was very sweet and gracious and then wrote:

I think Jeff is right. You would not make a very good spy.

See? He's a super cool guy. But sorry, ladies, last I heard, he's no longer single.

When Failing Isn't Funny

I tell this story as an icebreaker when I'm teaching workshops on relational boundaries. People laugh pretty hard, even if they saw the punch line coming. The audience feels sorry for me in my ridiculous humiliation, and some can even relate, having themselves sent emails or texts to the wrong person. I have no problem taking a bullet for the sake of loosening up the audience. I'm about to hit them with some challenging truths. The least I can do is start with open confession.

But here's the thing, friends: that kind of authenticity is easy for me because I'm a ham. Also, it's a confession that has been spun into an amusing anecdote. No one got hurt, and I'm not the bad guy; I'm just lame and silly and endearing in a Lucille Ball kind of way. (My husband disagrees, by the way. He thinks I should be really embarrassed about this story.)

But the next level of authentic is to confess this: I sometimes insert myself into people's lives in unhealthy ways. My tendency to send texts to the wrong people by accident (this is not the only time this has happened) is not the real issue. In the situation above, my pride and desire to be in control had made me believe that I not only would, but had the right to, choose a better man for my soon-to-be-single friend than she could choose for herself. I was far too invested in her life, to the neglect of my own family, and I was playing God in lots of ways. I even hid the Goodie setup from my dear husband because I knew he would disapprove, and I told myself lies about it: Jeff's disapproval was silly, and what I was doing was harmless, kind, and fun. But I knew in my heart that Jeff was right. It was too soon to be encouraging my friend to be interested in other men, and it was not my business anyway. Even when I got caught by Goodie in that text, I didn't tell my husband until months later, when I was readying to tell the story on stage.

I tell this story now to illustrate two important points: First, which is already obvious, is that I have issues, and I'm working on them. Second, is that it's possible to fake authenticity, to tell just enough about ourselves to seem like we're being humble and honest. Telling a seemingly humble story on stage is one thing; inviting you into my life and letting you see me fail, even while I'm failing, is something totally different.

We can fool each other by sharing just enough of our foibles to seem "real." Most of us shy away from going to the next level of confessing our flaws to each other and even spending enough time together to actually see each other struggling. That next level is what allows for real growth and strong bonds to form with our closest girlfriends, the kind of bonds that can heal our hearts and support us for the rest of our lives.

Authenticity Is the Beginning of Friendship

Being authentic means we allow people to really know us: what we believe and value, what makes us happy and what makes us angry, what we are good at, and where we are struggling. We not only receive confidences, but we also disclose the major circumstances of our own lives because when others know us, they can love the real people we are inside—or not. They may decide we're just not their cup of tea, and that's okay. That revelation brings freedom to relationships.

When we're authentic, we don't style ourselves as more competent or together than we really are. We don't constantly put romantic pictures of ourselves and our spouses on social media when we may be fighting constantly at home. If we're a Republican, we don't pretend to be more liberal to please our liberal friends (or vice versa). Being inauthentic is a barrier to healthy relationships because in some senses, it's manipulative. When we haven't revealed who we really are, we've lured each other into the relationship under false pretenses. Inauthenticity hurts both parties. It's so much work to hide who we are that there isn't room to be truly loving to one another. Women are particularly prone to being inauthentic about our life's circumstances because so many of us are afraid to show what our lives are really like behind closed doors.

Almost ten years ago, one of my best friend's husbands was carrying on a long-term affair. I suspected something was off for months before she told me about it. We had been friends for several years at this point, and one day, she hinted at what was going on. She didn't say it outright, but I knew her and understood what was really happening. The next week she had us over for dinner. Alone with her in the kitchen, I remember whispering, "What are we doing here? Am I supposed to pretend everything is okay while he's cheating on you?" She tried to take it back, to say it wasn't happening, because the fact was, she still kind of *did* want to pretend that everything was okay (and who can blame her?). Me—or anyone—knowing the truth meant she would have to face it in a way she hadn't before.

And that, friends, is the *scariest* part of being authentic. Because once the reality of our circumstances is known by others, we are pushed out of our own denial and likely will be pushed into dealing with it. But this is also the absolute *best* part of letting people see our real selves and our real lives. It gives our friends the power to encourage and stand with us, to hold us accountable to doing what is right. Authenticity is so important to understand; it's so important to accept as the foundation of healthy friendships, that without it, the other two components of this book—encouragement and accountability—won't be possible.

Pretending Takes a Lot of Energy

Loving and being loved by others is my favorite part of being a human being. It's also the hardest, most exhausting thing I do on a daily basis. This doesn't mean I'm brave necessarily. I'm just committed to my relationships—and, well, I'm too inept at keeping secrets to hide much. But I'm grateful God made me this way because big secrets can be a barrier to friendships.

In the situation above, my friend was enduring a lot of pain and confusion while she hid the secret of her husband's affair from those closest to her. She loved her friends (and her husband and children), but her ability to act loving, to be free in her relationships, was severely handicapped by the energy she was spending to hide the truth. Before she'd shared it with me, I went to her with something she'd said that had hurt my feelings, and she said, "If you had any idea what was going on in my life, you wouldn't be asking me for anything." But once she told me what was really going on in her home, everything changed. Not only did our friendship survive and thrive, but I, along with other safe women she let into the real issues of her life, helped her find the courage to set boundaries and deal with reality. And I'm thrilled to report that this friend is still married. She and her husband both went through an extensive period of counseling and recovery—both individually, in Christian community, and together. He fully repented and she fully forgave him. They continue to be some of our best friends.

The truths we are tempted to hide might not be quite as dramatic, but they can still hinder our relationships.

Have you ever . . .

- Acted like you had more money than you really did? Or pretended to be "okay" financially when you were actually worried about debt or making ends meet?
- Pretended to be healthy when you were enduring chronic pain or an illness?
- Presented yourself as a perfect, organized, joyful mother when you really felt you were just holding your head above water?
- Pretended to be really sure about Jesus when in fact you were struggling with doubts?
- Acted like you were happy and grateful when you were grieving or struggling with depression?
- Hid from your friends the wayward actions of a prodigal child or the pain of a fractured relationship with your adult children?
- Pretended to like something (a food, an activity, an event) because other people did and you didn't want to hurt their feelings or seem too different from them?

- Regularly made excuses not to do something your friends invited you to do instead of telling them the real reason you didn't want to come?

This kind of inauthenticity will always be a barrier to loving and being loved. I have known women who do all of these things. Some of them I've done myself. In every case, I've seen the relationships suffer from confusion, discouragement, loneliness, and lack of love.

I have a girlfriend who developed a lovely friendship with her neighbor. They spent a lot of time in and out of each other's houses for several years until my friend moved across town. After that, her old neighbor would make plans to get together, but then would cancel at the last minute. Just as their friendship was nearing a breaking point, the neighbor finally confessed that she had a terrible phobia of driving, about which she felt really ashamed. My friend was relieved—and gracious; she was so glad to know her neighbor wasn't rejecting her companionship. And she was grateful to be trusted with the truth.

Recently, a friend invited me to a night out in an Escape Room, a place where a group of friends are locked in a room together and have to solve puzzles in order to be let out. Instead of agreeing to it when I really didn't want to, or pretending I was just too busy, I said, "No way. I'm claustrophobic and being locked in a room is my personal nightmare; I won't go in mazes either." (Thank you, *The Shining*.) Because I chose authenticity and shared with my friend the reasons I declined, she knew I was rejecting the activity, not her. This not only increased love and trust in our relationship but also gave her permission to share her issues with me, being confident that I would accept her no's and her reasons for them. Now neither of us tries to hide. We can be authentic about what we like and don't like, and about what scares us, even if it seems silly to others.

Intimacy Is Like a String Bikini

But we need to be wise in our sharing. Being authentic doesn't mean bringing the whole iceberg out of the water in every social situation. Take it from me, a chronic oversharer if ever there was one. I don't want to send you out into the world with the most treasured desires of your heart, deepest secrets of your past, and most painful struggles of your present set out on a tray like samples at Costco. Why? For two reasons: I don't want you to get hurt unnecessarily. And I don't want you to freak people out by telling too much too soon.

As you seek authentic relationships, it's important to understand the difference between *intimacy* and *authenticity*. If authenticity is like wearing a dress without Spanx, intimacy is like wearing a string bikini. Both show your imperfections; one is just showing a lot more than the other. No one would call you "inauthentic" for coming to work wearing pants, but they also wouldn't praise you for being "real" if you came to a staff meeting in really short, skimpy running shorts, à la Will Ferrell in one of my all-time favorite *SNL* skits. It doesn't matter how flawless your body is. You could be Jessica Alba. Simply put, your booty should not be bare in the office.

My point is that some parts of our authentic selves and our stories can only be shared at appropriate times. Trauma, being abused as a child, financial hardships, significant losses, mental health issues, wayward children, a cheating spouse, and other aspects of our inner lives are not shameful. They are, in fact, intimate and worth guarding because they shape the precious heart that beats in your chest, a heart that God loves and died to redeem. Not everyone you meet deserves to know the inner workings of your heart and the private details of your story, and not everyone is equipped to receive these confidences.

I love that word *confidence* because it carries positive

connotations. I believe that in order to share confidences, we should have some confidence in the person with whom we share them. If we don't understand this truth, then our deepest fear might become realized—that is, if people really knew us, we would be "too much," too overbearing with our sharing. If we open up too soon or don't choose our confidants carefully, then the other person may turn and run or, worse, will give us a bunch of ill-informed input that will leave us feeling wounded and confused. Psychologists call this re-wounding; and it can make us afraid to be vulnerable in the future if those we trust with our inner lives hurt us again by reacting poorly.

Though my friend whose husband had an affair probably with-held her confidences from her closest friends for too long, imagine another less-than-ideal scenario. She's sitting on the side of the soccer field watching her child play in the game. She meets some other nice soccer moms, and as they're getting to know each other and sharing a bag of trail mix they borrowed from the kids' snack bag, my friend says, "Yeah, things are pretty rough right now. My husband has been cheating on me for the last six months." All the soccer moms stop chewing and look at each other with wide eyes. A particularly kind soul may move closer to my friend and might even put a hand on her arm compassionately. But most likely, my friend's revelation is a red flag to the other soccer moms, not because her troubled marriage disqualifies her from being their friend, but because she doesn't understand the art of authenticity.

There are some things we can share right away and some truths we should ease people into. In the previous anecdote, it was too early for my friend to talk about her marriage struggle in only the first hour of meeting new acquaintances. Those moms did not know who she really was. They didn't know who she had been in the past or how the past had shaped her. Moreover, they hadn't shown them-selves trustworthy to receive such confidences.

I love the way my friend and author David Zailer explained being authentic in a lecture: "Being an authentic, integrated person doesn't mean that all your most intimate thoughts and sins are *public*, but that you have a *community* in which you don't have secrets. Someone has to know the whole story!" (emphasis mine).[1]

I've known some truly sweet women who are confused by this concept. They are trying to be authentic, but they share too much too soon in person, or even post it on the Internet, hoping to receive acceptance and affection. They share their secrets like a dare: "Here is the weirdest/darkest/saddest part of my life. Will you love me? Or will you run?" People they've just met don't know how to respond to these disclosures, so it becomes a self-fulfilling prophecy of their worst fear that no one will love their authentic selves. If they had done a little more groundwork and spent a little more time developing the friendships before sharing these parts of their stories, they might have gotten a much different result.

The Big Secret to Making Authentic Friends

Long before I had friends whom I texted in bathrooms, I had to learn the importance of spending time getting to know my friends—and letting them get to know me. In the process, I endured many seasons of loneliness, pain, and confusion, and I lost friendships I'd thought would last for the long haul. In that difficult season, I remember thinking, *Why doesn't someone come to our mother's group and teach us how to make friends?*

Five years later, I was surprised when God called *me* to do it. I'd been developing a speaking platform to young mothers' groups, and a topic on my booking website attracted a good bit of attention. Dozens of churches hired me to deliver my talk, "All My Friends

Have Issues," to their women's groups. Another five years later, I was on the schedule at the MOPS International Leadership Convention (otherwise known as MomCon) for the same topic. Over one thousand women came to my workshops, and at the end of each session, I asked anyone who was feeling lonely or in need of discernment about a tough friendship to raise her hand so I could pray for her. At least one quarter of the room put their hands up.

In the workshop, I shared a picture of all my J's, taken at my fortieth birthday party. In the Q&A portion, one of the women wanted to know if all my friends were friends with each other, like on *Friends*. The answer was and still is no. It would be nice, though. I love that show, despite its canned laughter and sexual innuendo (which I didn't notice until I tried to watch reruns on Netflix with my daughters). *Friends* shaped a generation's vision of what friendship could be. In my favorite episode of all ten seasons (quoted at the beginning of this chapter), we learn that Monica has eleven categories for her bath towels, Joey wanted to be a space cowboy when he grew up, and Michael Flatley, Lord of the Dance, scares the "bejeezus" out of Chandler. In the show, the friends are always together and they don't have any other friends, which is about as realistic as their amazing hair and enormous apartments. But we bought in because they have what we want: someone who knows our histories, oddities, and pet peeves—and still loves us deeply.

Whenever I speak on this topic, I hear variations of this simple, heartbreakingly vulnerable inquiry: "How do I make friends?" or "How do I even start to get to know people?"

If you've found that friendships with other women are really hard, then you're not alone. In her book *The Secrets Women Keep*, Dr. Jill Hubbard lists the top fifteen secrets women keep based on her research and experience on the national talk show *New Life Live!* with Stephen Arterburn. In the top fifteen is this: friendship isn't easy. She wrote:

The secrets women are carrying about friendship tend to fall into two general categories. The first is the lack of fulfilling female friendships, and the biggest reason for this is our lack of time to nurture and invest in relationships with other women. . . . The second type of secret women keep about friendship is how intense female relationships can be and the depth of the pain we feel when they go wrong. Betrayal, competition, and backbiting among women can cause rifts as devastating as the breakup of a long-standing love relationship, including marriage.[2]

In my workshops, I try to answer "How do I make friends?" in forty-five minutes. I'm going to give you the answer in much more detail throughout this book, but it all hinges on three scary, risky, and time-consuming steps:

1. **Make making friends a priority.** We're all busy, but don't let that be an excuse.
2. **Leave your house.** You can't form a close friendship without spending some face-to-face time with each other.
3. **Invite people into your house.** Letting people see how you actually live and where you live will foster authenticity and comfort like nothing else can.

Making Friends in the Flesh

I love social media and I use it daily. But it tricks me into feeling like I have connected with other people when I really haven't. And it does this to all of us. We are sitting at home with our toddlers at our feet or we're in our beds at night, scrolling through our cell phones, and we crave human interaction. We check Facebook or Instagram and that hungry growl for connection in our soul feels slightly appeased when, in reality, we are as underfed spiritually and relationally as we would be if we chewed a piece of gum for nourishment. We haven't given anything beyond the click of a mouse, and we haven't had to sacrifice any other activities to do it.

We must be willing to sacrifice our time so that we can get to know each other and not just read about each other. Texting as a primary way of getting to know people isn't enough either because none of us are that good at *telling* others who we are. We usually just tell people who we *wish* we were and who we *think* we are (which is sometimes worse than we are, sometimes better). Texting is also an easy way to misinterpret tone, as a recent article in *Psychology Today* states: "It can be very difficult to distinguish humor and sarcasm from anger and criticism over text."[3] Experts recommend not using texting as a primary medium of communication until you understand each other well.

Because we're all a little afraid that others will cut us out of their lives after finding us to be imperfect, our tendency is to hide our flaws and struggles. Countless studies have shown that looking at social media makes us feel this fear more acutely and increases our insecurity and competitive drives. Despite the fact that we know intellectually that we're seeing other people's highlight reels online, *Psychology Today* also reports that "we appear to have a natural propensity to trust that others are being honest with us. . . . When we engage on social media and our propensity to trust is met with overt lying and less than honest presentations, it can be problematic because we internally presume that what is presented is true. That people are naturally as good-looking as their photos appear on a daily basis. That people's daily home life is as perfect as the pictures depict. That others have very few gut-wrenching struggles.

That people around us are in a habitual state of going on vacation, eating out, and parenting blissfully."[4]

Then we turn around and post our own highlight reels—image managing and ending up lonely.

The solution is to go old-school in our approach to friendship making. We have to be brave and engage with others in person: learning, taking risks, having fun, and being "naked" psychologically. And there is an added benefit to these activities: they are confidence-building.

In our young adult years, we have no idea how to do life yet, so we form unique bonds with friends in a way that we never have the opportunity to do again. Consider the *Friends* theme song: "Your job's a joke, you're broke, your love life's D.O.A." When I was in college, my girlfriends and I lived, worked, learned, and took risks with one another regularly. It was also the only time when I regularly saw my friends naked. Literally. My friend Josie and I roomed together in college for two years, and we still don't close the door when we go to the bathroom at each other's houses and often share a dressing room when we're shopping. On the other hand, despite seventeen years of friendship, my friend Jen and I didn't change clothes or go to the bathroom in front of one another until very recently, when we shared a hotel room at a convention where I was teaching. We are now the closer for it.

If you're still in your early twenties, you're in prime confidence-building season because learning and risk taking is likely a big part of your life, unless you're spending too much time in your dorm room on Instagram. But if you're older and more entrenched in routine, you have to put in a bit more intentional effort. I've been successful in established adulthood at forming friendships that unearth our issues and discover our strengths.

Some tips I've learned for making friends:

1. TAKE A CLASS, ASK SOMEONE TO TEACH YOU SOMETHING OR OFFER TO TEACH THEM SOMETHING.

Church is like a big classroom where we can meet new people, but unfortunately, it can also be a place we image manage more than anywhere else, which is not at all what God intended. To get around this, try some other classroom environments: cooking, dancing, rock climbing, or art. You can learn a lot about people by how they approach learning. Are they risk takers or are they cautious? Are they curious? Do they throw a haphazard dash of chili pepper in their wok during cooking class, or do they carefully measure it by the recipe? How do they act when their pot cracks in ceramics class? In Zumba, when the choreography gets tricky and they end up facing the wrong way, do they laugh and keep going, or do they berate themselves and give up?

Some of my best friends arc women I met in MOPS, which is churchy, but not actually church. Instead, it's like a topical parenting class that runs weekly from September to May. In a meeting, we would listen to speakers and then reflect on what we'd heard. Afterward, we would head out to the playground where we'd hand our hungry toddlers handfuls of Goldfish crackers as we finished our discussion. We learned about parenting together, then we went outside and actually *parented* together.

Parenting in front of an audience is nakedness in the extreme; nothing reveals character like coping with a kid having a big, hairy, snotty tantrum. (I think this also works at dog parks if your dog misbehaves.) We didn't find that we were doing everything the same, or that we were doing it perfectly, but we learned to support and accept each other. A few of the women I befriended in MOPS ten years ago are still my friends today, and we are counseling each other through the dangerous waters of parenting teenagers (so far, so good).

2. VOLUNTEER.

Helping with a cause in the community or a ministry at church lets you meet people with similar interests. (This works for meeting men, too, I hear.) You bond through helping others and you automatically have something to talk about. We see one another's strengths, weaknesses, and passions through doing something goal oriented. In a volunteer job, we can also see how potential friends handle taking directions, which is connected to their ability to cooperate and be humble.

3. DRIVE SOMEWHERE.

Before my daughters had hormones or crushes on the "wrong" sorts of boys, I gave them this advice: If a guy honks his horn a lot and yells at people in traffic, he has an anger problem and you shouldn't date him anymore. I tell them the Bible says, "Do not make friends with a hot-tempered person" (Prov. 22:24). You can test-drive (ooh, that pun was unintentional!) potential friends in the same way. When driving with a friend, I'm fascinated by who patiently drives behind a semitruck on the freeway, who runs yellow lights, and who cuts people off. When you're in a car together, you can help each other navigate and choose songs on the radio together. There are all kinds of opportunities to discover things about each other.

4. HAVE AN ADVENTURE.

Character is always revealed when you do something with people that is supposed to be fun and ends up being frustrating. Docking boats is good for this, as is putting chains on car tires in the snow, or playing sports with people who aren't really athletes. Hiking without a good map is also revealing. Jana and I learned a lot about each other when we were lost in a canyon and the vultures literally started circling overhead. (I discovered that Jana has a great attitude when she's lost and thirsty. Being dehydrated brings out her sense of humor. I, on the other hand, get vaguely hysterical when my physical needs aren't met, so make sure I've remembered my water if we hike together.) Amusement parks with small children are also excellent opportunities to bond. When someone's kid throws up or pulls down his pants and starts peeing on the plants outside of the Pinocchio ride in Disneyland, we're suddenly all in this together—or we aren't. The latter actually happened once, though it wasn't my kid (I have daughters, so it's difficult for them to pee in public). I think I proved to be extremely gracious through that circumstance. I loved my friend's no-nonsense response to it as well.

5. JOIN A SUPPORT GROUP.

If you are recently widowed or divorced, struggling with depression, struggling with infertility, battling an illness, or caring for someone with an illness, go find other people who are struggling in the same way. Doesn't that sound like fun? No, it doesn't actually. That sounds like maybe the riskiest, un-fun place to meet some safe, sane people. And you're right; it is risky. Support groups—whether through a twelve-step program, a hospital, or a church ministry—can be places where people with issues get stuck in their collective misery. But more often they are places of great healing, joy, and—I'm not kidding—laughter. I've met some of the healthiest people I know in groups and classes designed to help people with mood disorders and relationship problems. And in finding issues that we have in common, we find the lighter side of whatever it is we struggle with. When I started going to a support group for women who struggle with codependency (read on for more on that subject), I laughed harder than I did anywhere else in my life. I've made some incredible friends there. (And, by the way, support groups are also a place where it's totally acceptable to drop the bomb of your full reality on the first date.)

6. PLAY A GAME.

When my husband and I were first married, the leaders of our small group Bible study were really into game nights. It revealed who was competitive and who was not. Jen and I met in this group, and it turns out Jen's husband really doesn't like playing games but came anyway, which says a lot about him. And they learned something about me, which is that I am unbeatable at Taboo and Pictionary. (If we're going to be friends, you're going to want to be on my team or be okay with losing. Also, be okay with my lack of humility. I can't unlearn this about myself. Somewhere in the world, my friend Jodi is rolling her eyes at me right now because she actually beats me in Taboo, but only because she picks all the best players for her team—including my husband and my daughter.) Competition is a big revealer of character. I personally don't want to be close to a sore loser or—worse—someone who cheats.

7. GO SHOPPING OR OUT TO EAT.

I know it's a cliché, women shopping together. But if you want to know a lot about someone in a short time, go pick out clothes, shoes, or home accessories. You will learn how they make decisions (fast or slow, impulsive or research based, fearful or joyful), what colors they like and don't like, how they feel about their bodies, how they treat salespeople, whether they are messy or clean (check out the dressing room floor), if they have accepted or rejected Dave Ramsey's teaching on cash and credit cards, and how they handle money in general. Also, do they have essential friendship skills, like being able to give you honest advice, will they encourage your brave style choices without pushing their own style on you, and can they stop and start a conversation with multiple interruptions? Do they care about you as well as themselves?

In Marshall's, my friend Jodi (the Taboo champion) is like a determined, alert little terrier on my behalf. Long after I've given up finding the perfect pair of navy wedges in a size 9.5, she is still scanning the clearance rack and making salespeople "check the back." Meanwhile, Jen and I have discovered that the way we shop for clothes together is a metaphor for our entire spiritual relationship. She encourages me in my personal style (if it has a ruffle or vintage buttons, I'm in), as I encourage her in hers (think sleek and Calvin Klein), but we also challenge each other to try new things. Last time we went shopping, we each bought the same blouse (my style) and the same dress (Jen's style), but in different colors.

8. INVITE PEOPLE IN—LITERALLY.

I don't believe you can ever fully know someone until you've been inside their house (or apartment, or yurt, or wherever). And for this reason, many people don't invite others to their homes. They don't *want* their homes to reveal certain things about them. I can really relate to this. When I was a young mother, many of the friends I met at MOPS were much wealthier than I was, or so it seemed by the size of their wedding ring diamonds and vacation plans. I didn't want them to come to my house and have them see how small it was, but I did want to find something I could offer them. I invited them to a beautiful private park in my neighborhood, surrounded by a lake, complete with ducks and turtles. They showed up and were almost universally horrified that I had asked them and their unwater-safe toddlers to a playground surrounded by unfenced water. A half hour into the playdate, my three-year-old straight-armed a younger child right into the lake: the mucky, duck-poopy lake. That was a turning point. I had those moms to my small house the next time and offered them safe toys and hot coffee.

Now I love having people in my house. I'm no longer ashamed of the story my house tells about me, even if sometimes the story is, "I sort my husband's clean underwear in the living room while I watch TV and I haven't put them away yet." The story of my home is also about living within our means, expressing our creativity, embracing togetherness, and owning too much vintage stuff from garage sales. My sewing machine is usually on the table. My kids' school papers are on the chairs. My husband is almost totally not in evidence because he's so neat. I believe this environment helps people relax and let their guard down because women have told me all kinds of things on our third friendship date when they're in my house, things that just wouldn't have come out at a table in Starbucks. I love to be invited into someone else's safe space, too, and I don't think I have ever judged their sink full of dirty dishes or their furniture that doesn't match. I'm just glad to be allowed inside.

But this practice is real nakedness. My beloved sisters, some of you would never let someone you were just getting to know in your house. It's too messy, small, dirty, cluttered, shabby, and disorganized. Or it's too big and well-appointed and you're embarrassed of your material blessings. Or perhaps the story your home tells is more serious than that. It tells a story of financial hardship, unemployment, obsessive compulsion, addiction, an abusive spouse, or a child that has gone off the rails. It might tell a story of struggling with depression or feeling overwhelmed. And I realize that what we're talking about here, in this book on making and being friends, is about much, much more than finding someone to go shopping with. It's about facing our deepest issues. When we can't let people into our homes, we can't let people into our lives, and that is a tragic state of affairs. It's also solvable, I promise.

If that's your story, sister, know that *I know* I'm asking you to do something incredibly brave. If you're in the "no one is walking into my house" category, that's a sign that someone *needs* to be let in. I'm asking you to carefully, slowly maybe, tell the truth about yourself to someone. In her book *The Secrets Women Keep*, Jill Hubbard suggests first sharing your secrets with yourself, then God, and then, if possible, a trusted professional counselor. Finally, share with a friend.

> Sometimes there is somebody close to you who deserves to know this truth about you. In other cases, you may have a close friendship that hasn't grown because of your inability to be vulnerable and transparent, and you decide to take this person into your confidence.[5]

I'm praying that wherever you are in your authenticity with your friends, you will take the next step to go deeper, and then the next, and the next, until you have women in your life with whom you have actual intimacy. I pray that through the risk of making your relationships more real, God honors your courage. Because you need and deserve someone you can call from a bathroom stall. I believe God wants to give that to you.

Chapter 2

NUTS AND GIFTS

Authenticity and Self-Awareness

> I like for narrators [in books] to be like the people I choose
> for friends, which is to say that they have a lot of the same
> flaws as I. Preoccupation with self is good, as is a tendency
> toward procrastination, self-delusion, darkness, jealousy,
> groveling, greediness, addictiveness. They shouldn't be
> too perfect; perfect means shallow and unreal and fatally
> uninteresting.
>
> —ANNE LAMOTT, *BIRD BY BIRD: SOME*
> *INSTRUCTIONS ON WRITING AND LIFE*

About ten years ago, I was sitting in a workshop for people who struggle with anxiety and depression, and the lecturer said something that actually caused me more anxiety. My note-taking hand started to shake when he said, "One of the best weapons that you have in your arsenal against mental health crisis is a network of safe, sane friends."

Sitting next to me was Jana, a friend I met in MOPS and at that time a co-journeyer in the world of depression recovery. We looked at each other and knew the same thought was passing through our minds.

I'm crazy, and you're crazy. And that's why we're both here. Uh-oh.

Still in the workshop, I flashed back to a recent coffee night with another one of my best girlfriends. As usual, we parsed out the minute details of our most recent family conflicts and their possible childhood origins while sharing a piece of coconut cake. If a stranger at the next table had been paying attention, he might have thought he was listening in to a therapy session with two patients and no doctor.

Sitting there with Jana, reflecting on navel-gazing coffee dates with friends, I panicked. My friends weren't sane. Neither was I. Among my nearest and dearest, we joked that mutual craziness was what brought us together. We shared a little OCD, some codependence, a few compulsions, and more than a dash of irrational fears. We had troubles with our children, troubles in our marriages, trouble with money and with our mothers-in-law. We had trouble setting boundaries, trouble saying no to bad things and yes to good things. Some of us were compulsively neat and always early, and some of us were really disorganized and chronically late. The list went on.

So, what should I do now? Do I call off these relationships and go into the world in search of someone totally together who is willing to take me on as a charity case? I began making mental lists while in the workshop, and I was literally starting to sweat. Just having had my second baby, I'd spent the last year overcoming postpartum depression, so I thought, *I cannot go out and find a bunch of new friends right now.*

Then the lecturer provided blessed clarity. "Safe and sane," he said, "is someone who is honest, willing to admit their own faults, able to both give and take from the relationship, and above all, interested in personal growth. All of these were outlined by Christian psychologists Henry Cloud and John Townsend in their brilliant book *Safe People*."[1]

I breathed a sigh of relief.

Only a few months before, I had been asked a question in a game called Girl Talk: "What one characteristic do all your best friends share?" My answer had not been "anxiety" but "self-awareness." In other words, my friends and I *know* we have issues.

Having followed the principles for finding and investing in friendships that I described in the last chapter, and despite my ongoing struggle with depression, I was blessed to have a handful of humble friends, each of whom were deeply committed to growing in their friendships, work relationships, marriages, motherhood, and in their faith. Those friendships continue to this day, and it's fabulous to be around these women because they are always experiencing some new self-revelation and I get to witness it and, more often than not, learn from it as well.

I went home the night of the workshop and asked my husband, "Honey, do I have issues?" Jeff, who obviously adores me and thinks the sun rises and sets in my big brown eyes, laughed his head off. Later, he said that was one of the most ridiculous questions ever asked in the history of human interaction. Well.

One doesn't like to generalize about so many people at once, but I believe the world is not divided into those who have issues and those who don't, but rather, into those who *know* they have issues and those who don't. Or, to be even more specific, into those who can admit they have issues and those who can't.

In any relationship—friendship, romance, or otherwise—there

comes the point when some major weirdness is revealed. And I'm not talking just slumber-party kind of revelations, like the girl who talks in her sleep or has to brush each of her teeth the same number of times. I mean like significant personal quirks, dysfunctions, and even experience with destructive sin patterns. You go shopping, you take classes, you hike without water, and stuff comes up. None of the getting-to-know-you exercises in the last chapter will help you meet the perfect woman—because she isn't out there. Instead, they will help you get to know people as they really are and love them despite—and sometimes even because of—their quirks, struggles, and the obstacles they've overcome.

Way back in the perfectionism of my twenties, I was more tempted to hit the eject button when I reached the "issues" stage in my friendships. But now, after years of adventuring together, I've got the goods on a few girlfriends of mine. But you know how I feel about that? *Privileged.* I'm very blessed to have the kind of friendships where women let me in on their inner lives, close enough that I'm privy to their doubts and anxieties, their character defects, and the bad habits they're trying to break. I'm blessed, as well, by their deepest joys and triumphs. And they know about me too. Recently I confessed what I felt was a major but somewhat concealed character flaw to two of my best friends, and they both said, separately, "You know, I already knew that about you." But they liked me better because I could see it in myself.

At the same time, I've become more discerning about who I let close to my heart. I come back to the basic "safe and sane" requirement I learned ten years ago: if you've got issues but don't want to admit it or, worse, don't want to try to change at least a little, good luck and Godspeed because we cannot, at this time, share deep soul connection. However, if you ever change your mind and feel like coming clean, let me know. We'll save you a spot at our table.

You Have to Know Your Issues to Share Your Issues

Much more recently, my friend Jen (you should probably make a note of her; she comes up a lot) decided to start a new round of therapy. For her first appointment, she grabbed a folder from her desk drawer and stuffed her notes about her life history and current pressing issues into it—in other words, the reasons why she was going to therapy. Only on the way to the therapist's office did she notice it was labeled "Nuts and Gifts."

When she sent me the picture, I texted, "Sounds about right." Boy, did we laugh. (Later, I asked what was in that folder. She said it had contained recipes that she makes and gives to friends and neighbors at Christmas. Apparently, those foods involve nuts.)

As I write this little anecdote, I am flooded with gratitude. First, that I have such a dear friend, whom I met in a couples' Bible study nineteen years ago when we were both newlyweds without kids, and we were those girls in Bible study who said slightly inappropriate things. Secondly, that Jen is the kind of person who goes to therapy, and not in a Woody Allen, I-have-a-weekly-appointment-with-my-analyst-and-never-get-better kind of way but in a productive, life-has-just-revealed-some-new-challenges-I-might-not-have-the-skills-for-so-I-better-get-equipped kind of way. I adore her commitment to mental and spiritual excellence, which makes her a great friend, wife, mom, and witness for Jesus.

Third, and possibly my favorite reason I am grateful, is that I know almost everything—or at least the outline of everything—she has written in that file.

Though I met Jen in her twenties, I know what her childhood was like, which kid she was in the birth order, and which siblings she feels closest to. I know about her parents' marriage and how it affects the way she relates to her friends and family today. I've heard the stories about things that scared her, possibly scarred her a little, and shaped her from her early years. I know that she was a cheerleader in high school (she made JV but not varsity and it still bothers her). I know how she met her husband and where he proposed and how she felt about it. All these things happened before we ever met.

I can know all these things about Jen because she knows them about herself. Safe, sane friends seek to understand themselves and their own stories. One of the things that makes me feel most confident in Jen is that she regularly prays this courageous prayer: "Show me the truth about myself." She is one of the strongest planks in my protective fence of friends because she's aware of both her weaknesses and her profound strengths. You can't be honest if you don't know the truth, so I earnestly seek to be a safe friend in this way too. Because when we have a lack of self-awareness of our character, or big blind spots about our past and its effect on our present, then authentic connection is difficult because we act and react to people and situations without knowing why.

The kind of authenticity we're talking about in this book is so much more than being able to answer a question honestly when we're asked (which, frankly, can be challenging enough). Instead, this book focuses on the kind of authenticity that brings long-term, deep closeness and the ability to support each other in the most important pursuits of our lives. To do that, we need to understand not just what our friends like and *are* like, who and what they *don't* like, what they are good at and where they struggle, but also *why*. We first need to understand this about ourselves.

Some Issues Go Way Back

There's a saying often used in therapists' offices and twelve-step support groups: "If you're hysterical, it's historical." Milan and Kay Yerkovich, authors of *How We Love*, a Christian book on attachment theory and relationships, write about this principle at length.[2] Attachment theory postulates that your earliest relationships with your parents and/or primary caregivers shape the ways you relate to people in the present. What bothers you in the present is probably triggering some pain you experienced in the past. For example, if your parents or caregivers were inconsistent about showing up when they said they would, often leaving you waiting, then as an adult, you might feel exaggerated anxiety or even a sense of abandonment when one of your friends is regularly late to meet for coffee. Or if you grew up being made fun of for being "needy" or "too sensitive," then you might feel an overwhelming sense of rejection when you ask a friend for a favor and she says no. Positive feelings can be triggered by the past too: much of what we love and what makes us feel safe we learned as kids.

How We Love focuses on marriage relationships, but when I was recently a guest on a *New Life Live!* radio broadcast with Milan, he affirmed that their research and teaching were always intended to improve the quality of all relationships. The historical/hysterical principle is equally influential in friendships. One of the great blessings of long friendships is that you might actually have witnessed the life events that shape your friends' personalities: strengths, affinities, flaws, and fears. But it works just as well to be told about them. We need compassion for our friends in order to love them well in the long run, and understanding what pain may have shaped their lives helps us do that. Sharing these things about ourselves can also be deeply healing. Kay Yerkovich writes about sharing significant memories from her past with her husband, "As I shared, I realized what a caring, compassionate listener can do to help us discover the impact of an event on our lives."[3]

You've heard the expression, "Be kind, because everyone you meet is fighting some sort of battle." With my closest friends, I have had the opportunity to learn their back stories and what battles they have faced, including their worst fears. When they're over-reacting to something, I might think, *Oh, this is reminding you of when your father left. It's reinforcing the lie that everyone will leave you.* But I, being the wise person I sometimes am, don't say those thoughts aloud right away. First Peter 4:8 says, "Above all, love each other deeply, because love covers over a multitude of sins." Being understanding about our friends' issues is even easier if we literally understand why they have them.

Be Brave, Be Authentic

The Psalmist says, "Behold, you delight in truth in the inward being" (Ps. 51:6 ESV), which is another way of saying that God wants us to be honest and authentic down to our very core. For this reason, I try to understand as much about myself as God is willing to reveal to me. And then, I try to authentically share it with my girlfriends. Only then can they love the real me.

But this is a huge risk to take with real, regular women. It's possible that this soul sharing could go horribly wrong. For one, they might not be as fascinated with my introspection as I am or, worse, they could reject the real me when I show them the full picture. But more often than not, the reaction I've received is an outpouring of grace. It's easier to be gracious to me when my friends know I sincerely need it. And secondly, when they understand some of the things I have experienced and overcome, they are more willing to cut me some slack. I, in turn, do the same for them, as much as I can with God's help.

For authenticity to work, brave conversations are required with a mutual sharing of ourselves, because, remember, safe and sane people give as well as take. If you've got a pretty good friend already, get a cup of coffee or put on your walking shoes, then set out, ready to share on some of these heady subjects:

- Your families of origin and childhood experiences
- Big moments when God "showed up" in your lives
- Past hurts that have shaped the way you relate to people in the present
- Current struggles you face in your workplaces and primary relationships (usually with your spouses, kids, siblings, or parents)
- Your character flaws and habitual sins
- Your deepest fears about yourselves and the future
- Your deepest desires and dreams for the future

Some of this is scary stuff to talk about, yet to be known on this level is one of the great rewards of life. It's also been of great benefit to my marriage. My husband also knows me on this level, but he's not as excited to talk about it as my girlfriends are. Nor is he as able to relate to some of my struggles. Having peers to relate to and process with takes a lot of pressure off our other relationships: husbands, boyfriends, parents, children.

Remember: we need to be wise in timing our sharing. I'm not suggesting you drop these bombs at lunch with coworkers in the conference room or during happy hour at girls' night out, because this is like PhD-level soul baring. Instead, open yourself to the possibility and potential of these ways of sharing yourself with others. And *take your time*. Look for opportunities to develop self-awareness and a desire to embrace others' journeys toward understanding themselves. We all have issues. By sharing them, we might be able to help each other feel less hysterical, no matter what our history.

Some Issues Are Deal Breakers

My friend Wendy and I have been close for a long time, so much so that we occasionally share our unfiltered and slightly unkind thoughts about others. (Don't judge. This is one of the greatest gifts of close friendships: you can say anything safely and know that it won't be repeated at times and places that will hurt others. Hey, we're real people. We aren't saints.) Wendy and I occasionally have discussed our deal breakers in a dating relationship. This is odd because we have both been married for decades, but that doesn't stop us from our hypothetical game. One of Wendy's deal breakers is this: If a man takes his sunglasses off his eyes and perches them on his forehead. Not on top of his head like a headband, because that's okay. But stuck on his forehead like he has an extra pair of eyes up there, which, to her, is unacceptable. We were lunching at a restaurant once where she saw a man who kept his sunglasses in that spot for his whole meal. That would have been it for Wendy. No second date.

For me, a deal breaker is when men back into parking spaces in a lot where everyone else has pulled forward. I hate it when I'm stuck in a crowded parking lot waiting for some guy to do an eighteen-point turn backward into a headfirst parking space so that when it's time for him to leave, he can zip right out. I can't figure out how wasting all this time at the beginning makes up for the few seconds of saved time at the end. If one of my dates did this but could laugh at himself when I asked him about it, we might be able to continue the relationship. If he staunchly defended his parking behavior, however, I'd be out.

The fact is I'm willing to put up with more small annoyances in a friend than in a life partner. (If my girlfriends want to back into their parking spaces, I can handle it because I drive with them less often than I do with my husband.)

We probably have deal breakers in friendships too. Ultimately, the only person who can judge what makes a friendship worth the risk is you, and your quirky deal breakers are likely different from mine. Both my daughters have been friends with girls who had quirks and qualities that I found annoying, but that didn't mean those girls were unsuitable friends for my kids. My kids found that the joy in spending time with those friends outweighed the small irritations. Observing this has given me new insight into my own relationships. It has made me realize that friendship is meant to be enjoyable. If I'm spending a lot of time with someone who really bugs me, that's not good for either of us. It would be better to release her so that she can befriend women who won't be rubbed raw by her quirks. And I certainly don't want you gritting your teeth as you bear my weirdness; if you don't like me, stop returning my texts. I'll get the picture eventually and find another friend.

On the other hand, I do believe that certain issues are deal breakers for all those who strive to have healthy, loving, safe, sane relationships. I don't like the term "toxic people" because I believe all people are capable of change. However, I do believe recognizing toxic relationship *patterns* is helpful.

Deal-breaker patterns will be described throughout the book and are found in the Reader's Guide at the end of the book for your reference. If you see some of your own traits in the deal-breaker sections, don't despair. And don't call up your girlfriends and tell them they'd be better off without you. Instead, keep reading, and pray for yourself. When we are willing to see our issues and work on them, God is faithful to complete the good work he began in us, because the ability to love and be loved is what he most wants for his daughters.

Chapter 3

PERFECTION IS FOR YO-YOS

Finding Wisdom Among Imperfect Women

The next best thing to being wise oneself is to live in a circle
of those who are.

—C. S. LEWIS

My friend Jodi's favorite thing to do when we're hanging out together
is to roll her eyes at me. I can tell when she's doing it even when we're
talking on the phone. The pause in dialogue is now so characteristic
of our conversations that I know she's taken this break to express her
exasperation with me by rolling her eyes. Jodi does this whenever
I reference the fact that I am no longer a perfectionist. She believes
that I am in deep denial or lying through my teeth.

I probably deserve this treatment, but not because Jodi is right.
I am in fact so recovered from my former slavery to perfectionism
that the twenty-five-year-old version of me would hardly recognize
the forty-one-year-old version. Instead, I deserve it because one
of the first times that Jodi and I hung out together, I called her a

pathological perfectionist. You probably understand how that might have made her defensive.

The occasion was this: Jodi had learned that I love to sew and had seen one of my favorite things to make, a garland of yo-yos. A yo-yo is a circle of fabric that is stitched and gathered by hand to create a simple rosette. They can be sewn onto quilts, or as an embellishment on a pillow, or end-to-end to make a garland. Jodi asked if I could teach her to make them (a great way to make friends is to teach them something, right?). In the course of our lesson, I confirmed what I had already discovered about my new friend. She is a person who likes to do things well and "right." Whereas I accepted in her work (as in my own) some uneven gathers and some stray threads, and despite my assurance that her yo-yos were just fine, she insisted on ripping many of them apart and starting over.

Hence the "pathological" remark.

Because Jodi is awesome, and by fortune and grace we have understood one another's hearts from early in our acquaintance, she continued to hang out with me after that and even came to love me as I do her. We met when our girls started kindergarten together, and they are now in the sixth grade. For years we have been engaged in this dialogue about what perfectionism really means.

One psychological definition of perfectionism is this:

> Normal perfectionists derive a very real sense of pleasure from
> the labors of a painstaking effort, while neurotic perfectionists
> are unable to feel satisfaction because in their own eyes they
> never seem to do things well enough to warrant that feeling of
> satisfaction.[1]

So perhaps, in the matter of yo-yos, Jodi is not actually neurotically or pathologically perfectionistic, but a "normal" perfectionist, someone with high standards who takes pleasure in doing things well. I have also seen her make scrapbooks. She is very, very attached to her ruler. And by the definition above, she's also right about me. I like excellence. I like to make things beautiful. I throw great birthday parties and dinner parties. I make a mean quilt. And I try to be intentional in just about every area of my life.

But I am no longer a pathological perfectionist: I give myself a break. Sewing—specifically quilt making—has helped me achieve this. I learned to make quilts twenty years ago and took to sewing like a duck to water. In my own unique way. I know someone whose happy place is the Nordstrom shoe department, and she feels giddy about even just the way it smells. That's how I feel when I'm near bolts of fabric in a quilt shop. I have a knack for choosing different colors and prints, but rarely have I bought a pattern and made it according to the instructions all the way through. I like to add my own touch to it, and the whole process just brings me joy.

In other ways, I was quite ill-suited for quilting. For example, cliché though it is, I'm a word girl and I don't like numbers. Or precision. Quilting involves a lot of measuring, cutting, geometry, and following rules. Like painters, who can't start out with cubism, you have to know some basic skills in sewing before you can riff. So the mathematical, step-by-step aspect of sewing was challenging.

My first teacher was my mathematically minded mother-in-law, Susan, who has been sewing her whole life. Susan is a great teacher, and she's a big fan of the seam ripper. Occasionally there was conflict when Susan gave me lessons. I would get frustrated with myself for not being precise and then frustrated with her for telling me to redo the things I had done wrong so that I wouldn't develop bad habits in the basics.

I eventually decided that if perfection was what was required in sewing, I would give it up. But I loved it too much to quit. So I made a radical decision to let many crooked seams lie. My motto became, "There's enough good in good enough," which I learned from a church friend named Brooks. My early work was a little wonky, but it got finished, and two decades later I have the skill to be more precise, just from practice. If I'd demanded perfection from myself at the beginning, I would have quit. By now, I have made quilts for just about every loved one in my life *and* their children. For my fortieth birthday last year, I had a needle and thread tattooed on my ankle: a testament to my lifelong desire to sew and sow love into the world.

Anne Lamott's description of perfectionism sounds about right to me:

> Perfectionism is the voice of the oppressor, the enemy of the people. It will keep you cramped and insane your whole life. . . . I think perfectionism is based on the obsessive belief that if you run carefully enough, hitting each stepping-stone just right, you won't have to die. The truth is that you will die anyway and that a lot of people who aren't even looking at their feet are going to do a whole lot better than you, and have a lot more fun while they're doing it.[2]

Perfectionism is the enemy of creativity. It's the enemy of risk taking. It's the enemy of new learning. And nowhere is perfectionism more destructive to our joy than in the matter of making and keeping friends.

I feel about friendship the way I do about quilting: I expect it to bring me joy, and so I stomach the risk of failure. Also, as in quilting, I lacked some essential friendship skills when I went out into the adult world. I thought I was good at honesty, but I had trouble recognizing dishonesty, both in myself and others. I both manipulated others and allowed others to manipulate me. I befriended anyone who seemed interesting, but I didn't know the first thing about how to tell if they were someone with whom it was safe to share my heart. Sometimes, even when I found safe, direct, self-aware people, I pushed them away because they didn't seem as exciting as the chaotic and dramatic ones. With others, when I came in contact with certain issues of theirs that triggered issues of *mine*, I took off running.

Something deep in us desires to know and be known. But when it comes to the details, or the hard work, we're ill-equipped and unprepared. This is all okay, though, because we don't come into the world knowing how to form honest, loving relationships. Our parents and caregivers—who are, in theory, the ones to teach us—maybe haven't got it figured out either. Perfectionism, therefore, the belief that flawlessness must be attained in ourselves and in others, will sabotage forming authentic relationships. All relationships carry risk: we have to try and fail and be willing to get our hearts broken, then learn and keep going. And as with sewing or any other worthy pursuit, we have to believe it's worth it. We have to believe that friendship will bring us joy.

Am I Being Judgmental or Discerning?

Perfection is for yo-yos, not people. We may eventually achieve perfect output in a presentation for work, or in sewing a pillow, or in baking a pineapple upside-down cake, but we will never find the perfect friend. But how imperfect is too imperfect? This is one of the essential questions of this book.

When I first became a mom, I had a vision of who my perfect best friend would be. She would live within walking distance, and our kids would be the same age and gender. She would come over to my house, and we would bake together. Then we would sit at the kitchen table and talk while our kids played happily on the floor with American-made wooden toys. While we talked we would find all kinds of common ground: We liked the same books, movies, and TV shows, and we wanted the same people to win on *American Idol*. We'd agree on major points of theology, politics, and disciplining children. Eventually, our husbands would meet and really like each other. We'd start having Sunday barbecues and taking family camping trips together. As the kids got older, our husbands would hang out with the kids while we went shopping (for fabric would be ideal, but shoes would work too) or out to eat at our favorite restaurant (the same one).

You're laughing now. But you've had similar fantasies, I bet.

The good news is that, fourteen years later, I have found that perfect friend, only she's five different people. As lovely as it would be to have the friend-equivalent of a wife—one woman who is biblically bound to stay in relationship with me and care for my needs—these social and spiritual needs have been met by a whole community of women, which is what God intended.

The real problem with my perfect friend scenario is that she is basically a blonde version of me, and if I'm being totally honest, I would prefer she be brunette because blondes intimidate me. (If you grew up in Southern California as a brunette, you'd understand.) What a humbling admission. Does it mean I believe I am the perfect friend? Or does it speak to the fact that what I really want is someone who won't challenge me, someone with whom I will never have any conflict?

I'm so glad God never granted me this request, because, frankly, if all my friends were just like me, I'd be a train wreck. Back in my perfectionistic twenties, I felt the same way about people that I did about fabric. I found them lovely and interesting, but unfortunately, I also wanted to make them mine, cut them up, and reform them into an image that worked for me. Being in relationships with women of differing skills, opinions, and interests who actually provoke me to consider where I might be wrong is what has kept me from being an insufferable person. Left to my own devices, or befriended by my doppelganger, all my bad qualities would get worse and my good qualities would not be needed.

And yet, there are such things as unreconcilable differences between friends. Though I don't want to be someone who disregards people too soon and takes off at the first sign of conflict, neither do I want to be in friendships in which conflict and annoyance are constants. I want joy and comfort in friendships.

In the movie *Julie and Julia*, the main character Julie and her best friend, Sarah, are dishing on a friend they don't like over martinis. It's one of my favorite scenes because it captures this aspect of female friendships so well.

"What does it mean about you if you don't like your
    friends?" Julie asks.
"Totally normal," says Sarah.
"Men like their friends," says Julie's long-suffering husband.
"Who's talking about men?" asks Sarah.[3]

Sarah and Julie are demonstrating some unhealthy habits here. They believe their friend in question is vapid and self-absorbed, and we see at other times in the movie that she hurts Julie's feelings with her self-centeredness. And yet, Sarah and Julie still call her a friend.

I think this may be a common experience among women, that we have at least one friend whose life decisions drive us crazy because they seem unhealthy and chaos producing, or who hurts our feelings over and over again. But we don't stop being friends with her. We just talk about her behind her back. (My husband is someone who holds me accountable to *not* do this.) I wish this were something that happened only among non-Christians, but it isn't.

Part of the problem for us as women is that when it comes to deciding who we should be spending time with, we are sometimes unsure if we're being judgmental (and perfectionistic) or if we're being discerning. We say to ourselves, *Everyone has issues, right? Who am I to say which ones have crossed a line?* I'd like to offer some solid advice from Proverbs 13:20 as a foundation: "Walk with the wise and become wise; associate with fools and get in trouble" (NLT). And also, "The righteous choose their friends carefully, but the way of the wicked leads them astray" (Prov. 12:26).

It would be healthier for Julie and Sarah, and us, to choose to spend time around women we believe are edifying and ethically upright. That's not selfishness; it's sincerity. And furthermore, it's wise.

Business philosopher and motivational speaker Jim Rohn said that we become the average of the five people we spend the most time with. The Bible also outlines this principle. Based on this research, then, our closest friends—let's say the closest three to five women in our lives—need to be women of wisdom. You will not agree with all your friends' decisions (we will cover this in depth in part three on accountability), but you should be pretty sure that they aren't fools, as the Bible defines them.

The Difference Between Flawed and Foolish

Fools and "simpletons" are defined throughout the book of Proverbs and are contrasted with people of wisdom and prudence:

- 1:22: How long will mockers delight in mockery and fools hate knowledge?

- 10:23: A fool finds pleasure in wicked schemes, but a person of understanding delights in wisdom.
- 12:16: Fools show their annoyance at once, but the prudent overlook an insult.
- 12:23: The prudent keep their knowledge to themselves, but a fool's heart blurts out folly.
- 14:1: The wise woman builds her house, but with her own hands the foolish one tears hers down.
- 14:3: A fool's mouth lashes out with pride, but the lips of the wise protect them.
- 14:7–9: Stay away from a fool, for you will not find knowledge on their lips. The wisdom of the prudent is to give thought to their ways, but the folly of fools is deception. Fools mock at making amends for sin, but goodwill is found among the upright.
- 27:12: The prudent see danger and take refuge, but the simple keep going and pay the penalty.

These verses paint a pretty clear picture (and for me, are convicting of some behaviors I could keep in check). A foolish person:

- acts without thinking carefully,
- speaks without knowledge or self-awareness,
- is reactive and short-tempered as a rule,
- disdains the moral law of God and other authorities,
- is dishonest,
- makes dangerous decisions that lead to chaos for herself and those around her, and
- refuses to apologize for wrongdoing.

In short, the fool lacks the qualities of a safe friend we defined in the first chapter:

- honest,
- willing to admit their own faults (their lack of knowledge, their issues, their hurtful behaviors),
- able to both give and take from the relationship, and
- interested in personal growth.

Being a fool or a simpleton isn't about IQ or education then. It's about attitude. Psalm 19:7 says, "The statutes of the LORD are trustworthy, making wise the simple." So foolishness is primarily an issue of having an unteachable, prideful heart. Being unteachable, or having what Jesus called "a callused heart" in the parable of sowing seeds, leads to disharmony in our own lives and the lives of others. Before having our hearts regenerated by the Holy Spirit when we accept Christ as our Savior, much spiritual wisdom will sound like foolishness to us (1 Cor. 1:18). But even after we are saved, we can still be foolish if we resist self-knowledge, God's leading, and the input of those around us. We can still act like fools and befriend them.

I don't even like typing the world *fool* and certainly don't like calling anyone a fool. It reminds me of how Jesus said in Matthew 5:22, "Again, anyone who says to a brother or sister, 'Raca,' is answerable to the court. And anyone who says, 'You fool!' will be in danger of the fire of hell." Ouch!

But here is an important distinction between the biblical definition of a fool and the name-calling that Jesus says puts us in danger of judgment:

> The term *raca*, spoken from a heart of contempt, implied utter worthlessness. Jesus was not saying that we cannot call the choices of another foolish. But to call someone "raca" was saying that this person was beyond the reach of God and therefore condemned

forever. To say, "You fool!" to a brother or sister in that day was the equivalent of saying, "Damn you!" to someone today.[4]

Determining that someone is an unsafe friend for a season—or forever, if they don't show fruit of repentance or signs of personal growth—is not the same as condemning them or calling them worthless. Neither is it deciding that they are unworthy of any other relationships and warning people accordingly, which reflects another question I'm often asked from the audience: "Can someone be unsafe for me but safe for someone else?" I get what they're asking. If Jesus said, "Don't throw your pearls to swine or they will be trampled underfoot," then isn't it possible that someone is simply a swine, which seems worse than a fool? My response is I don't believe "once a swine, always a swine." Regardless of someone's issues, the Bible is pretty strict about staying away from gossip; so don't go warn the women in your Bible study to stay away from the friend you need a break from.

Jesus commanded us to show love to the world. However, I know he also loves *us* dearly. He doesn't expect us to have our hearts trampled, tainted, or influenced by close friendship with fools.

That's why it's crucial to get to know people in real life and real time, as I outlined in the first chapter. When we see evidence of chronic anger, foolishness, pride, reckless decision-making, and unteachable hearts in potential new friends, we can do as Proverbs tells us: "The prudent see danger and take refuge" (27:12).

There's Enough Good in Good Enough

Even in our assessment of foolishness, we should let go of perfectionism, give grace, and take a long view of things.

Among my dearest, enduring friends, each of us have had semi-long stretches of insane behavior, times when we ran some aspect of our lives into the ground by continuing to do the same thing over and over again and expecting different results. All of us have shown signs of hardheadedness for a season, times when we just weren't learning what God was trying to teach us. Eventually God got our attention (often, he uses friendships to do it; more on that subject in part three). He worked out some major character defects in us, but it took some time. If your friend has been on a trajectory of wisdom and proactivity in her life but now seems to have gone off the rails, my suggestion is to wait it out, as many women have graciously done for me.

My church follows biblical principles in choosing elders who serve our congregation. Elders need to be wise people who consider their words and actions carefully. But they are still human. Last year our church appointed a restoration team to serve the elders, because they know that those who qualified at one point in their lives may run into difficulties over the years, as they carry the spiritual weight of our church; they may have prodigal children, their marriages could end up on the rocks. This restorative team is here to minister to those elders and their families; rather than calling them disqualified, the church will work to restore them. If our elders fear disqualification, why would they reach out for help or be authentic? The risk would be too great.

And that's why perfectionism ultimately kills friendships. When we're perfectionists, we give up too quickly on women who could be real gifts in our lives and who could teach us valuable lessons. When our friends are perfectionists, we tend to hide our authentic selves, fearing that they will give up too quickly on us. Let's look for teachability and humility in our friends first and foremost, taking as our motto, "There's enough good in good enough."

The Joy Factor

I'm so grateful that Jodi has stuck it out with me for the last six years, even though I called her pathological. I've come to know her as a wise woman who has proactive approaches to problem solving and is a loving and thoughtful mother. She's also one of my go-tos if I need perspective on an issue with my teenage daughter or advice about how to handle a sticky situation with my daughters' school administration.

But most of all, she has the final criteria of a good friend I want to highlight in this chapter. She's *fun*. I really enjoy being with her. She looks and can sing like Snow White and has the personality of Mary Poppins (she likes being called "practically perfect in every way"). She is also kind, insightful, hardworking, long-suffering, and smart. Unlike my perfect mirror-image friend at the beginning, we don't agree on everything. We don't even like the same actors (she doesn't find Ryan Gosling attractive, which shows she has real issues). But we have so much fun arguing about it. She makes me laugh, mostly at myself, and she lets me laugh at her. One of the joys of being with Jodi is that she always finds ways to let me know that she really likes *me*. There are plenty of people who don't; I'm glad she does.

Just days ago, I was telling her of my intentions for this chapter and asking her permission to tell our story. She, of course, rolled her eyes. I told her to feel free to put any objections to my perfectionist recovery in a public comment when the book comes out. While we were in the middle of this exchange, my ten-year-old came into the room and brought to my attention that her teacher conference was beginning in eight minutes; I had completely forgotten. Oh, did Jodi and I laugh as I ran upstairs to put on decent clothing; she agreed to stay at my house and watch our daughters while I went to the school.

"See," I said, as I ran back downstairs, "if I was a perfectionist, I'd be condemning myself for forgetting the conference, but I'm so recovered that I can simply laugh it off."

Perfection is for yo-yos. Demand perfectly even gathers and perfectly round results in your sewing as long as you have the time, will, and inclination to do so. By all means, set high standards for your pursuits: in crafting, career, parenting, friendship, marriage, and your relationship with God. But by no means set unrealistic expectations for yourself in friendship. Forgive and make allowances for each other and then notice your level of joy.

Chapter 4

I'M SO SENSITIVE

Hurt Feelings and Authentic Apologies

I'm so sorry that I didn't want your rather bulbous head
struggling to find its way through the normal-sized neckhole
of my finely knit sweater.

—FROM *SEINFELD*, "THE APOLOGY"

My friend Wendy is older than my mom (which she will be totally
fine with me saying in print). We met sixteen years ago when I
interviewed her for a magazine article on women who quilt in our
community. Wendy was part of a "friendship group" called The
Pinup Girls. Imagine a small-group Bible study, but instead of talking about Jesus and personal growth, they get together and eat and
drink and talk about sewing, fabric, sewing teachers, their families,
and personal growth. A year after my article came out, I ran into
these fun ladies, and they asked me to join. I accepted gratefully.
Over the years, our group gained and lost members and got a new
name—The Yo-Yos, which I obviously love—then eventually faded

out. But Wendy and I, who live less than a mile away from each other, have remained close.

Our friendship was first built on our mutual interest in sewing. We attended quilt shows together, shared our projects with each other, and I still steal fabric from her enormous stash. Over time, we discovered other mutual interests too. We're both passionate about learning and personal growth, following our hearts' desires, and entrepreneurship. For years, I went to her house every Tuesday to watch *American Idol*. Though we are decades apart, we share many similar worldviews and the same taste in pop music, and when she says things like, "That was my favorite song in high school," I enjoy responding, "That song came out ten years before I was born!" By choice, she never had children, but she loves mine and is like an extra "auntie" in their lives.

One thing Wendy and I do not agree on is politics. Once, after the most recent election, my daughter and I went over to Wendy's to visit. We were talking about how I was taking a social media fast because I was overloaded with other people's political opinions. Then I offhandedly expressed one of my opinions, gave Wendy a hug, and drove away. A week later, I realized I was out of a fabric I needed and called Wendy to ask if I could shop around for it in her quilting room. She said to come on over. But as we were sifting through her drawer of polka dot fabrics, she said, "I have to tell you something. I'm really mad at you."

"What? Why? Oh no!" was my reaction. Immediately I got that sick feeling in my stomach, like when you see police lights flashing behind your car and suddenly realize that you didn't come to a full stop at that last stop sign.

Wendy went on to say, firmly but with a break in her voice, what my political comment had meant to her, how she had felt judged, and how me making such an insensitive comment in front of my daughter hurt her even more—that I was teaching my daughter to judge and label people on the other side of the political street.

The knot in my stomach began to unclench, and a new feeling emerged. Gratitude. Here before me was a woman who loved me enough to tell me the truth, to give me a chance to apologize, and to heal a hurt between us. (And she was letting me borrow fabric even when she was mad at me!) Wendy had been debating within herself whether to tell me how I'd upset her, and when I called to ask for a favor she took it as a sign that she had to speak up.

We had a wonderful, frank conversation about what I had meant (not what she thought I'd meant), but I owned the thoughtlessness of my remark. I thanked her for the opportunity to clear things up. Later that day, we texted back and forth about our mutual thankfulness for our friendship, and Wendy said something the spirit of which I'll never forget, even if I don't remember the exact wording: "I'm grateful for the lesson I've learned in life, that rather than sitting on our hurt feelings, we should be brave and share them rather than letting resentment build up."

Amen and amen.

I'm grateful for that lesson in Wendy's life too. It helps me to realize that, though thirty years older than I am, she still wrestles with when to speak up about hurt feelings and when to keep quiet and hope the feelings simmer down. (It reminds me of Proverbs 12:16: "Fools show their annoyance at once.") I also love the general principle by which she lives: that telling the truth about our feelings is essential to our relationships.

Making Peace, Not Keeping It

I titled this chapter "I'm So Sensitive" because I spend time with a lot of women—as a teacher, small group leader, friend, school volunteer, and mother of daughters—and I've come to believe that many of us are afraid of appearing "too sensitive." Deciding to speak up when we feel hurt and sharing our hurt feelings in appropriate ways is actually harder than responding graciously when someone tells us we've hurt them. But healthy relationships, as Wendy shows us, are not just about being able to admit when we've wronged someone but also about admitting when we feel we've been wronged.

I grew up in the conflict-adverse culture of the middle-class, American Protestant church. In that culture, women spend a lot of time and effort being nice. Nice, gentle, kind, patient, long-suffering, humble, and peace loving. Outwardly, we were pretty good at that. We never yelled at each other in our Sunday school class or in our Bible study. At potlucks, we brought our food and didn't want to be the first one in line to eat it. We held open doors for others and volunteered our time.

But inside, many of us were smoldering against family, friends, church leaders, and others in our lives. We had hurt feelings and resentments; we remembered passive aggressive comments people made. And since we weren't equipped to handle honest and direct confrontation, we made passive aggressive comments back. Or we talked behind people's backs. Inside, we suffered from guilt that we were not as "nice" as we thought Jesus wanted us to be. After all, it was he who said, "Blessed are the peacemakers." We had achieved external peace (no one was throwing chairs a la Jerry Springer at Bible study or Thanksgiving dinner), but we didn't have peace in our hearts.

In her Bible study series *Living Beyond Yourself*, Beth Moore addresses this troubling condition among Christian women. She says there is a difference between being a peacemaker (Matt. 5:9) and a peacekeeper (spiritually unhealthy). Jeremiah 6:14 says, "They have healed the brokenness of My people superficially, saying, 'Peace, peace,' But there is no peace" (NASB). Moore teaches that we bring peace to life and relationships when we honestly and openly address feelings, wounds, and sin. Jesus himself said that he did not come to bring peace, but a sword. Truth may cause division. But unity based on denial of reality is not really peace at all.[1]

This concept is primary in Peter Scazzero's book *Emotionally Healthy Spirituality*, which asserts that we cannot have spiritual maturity without a healthy awareness of our emotions. In the book, he defines the top ten symptoms of emotional immaturity, and number seven is "spiritualizing away conflict." Scazzero writes, "I saw conflict as something that had to be fixed as soon as possible. Like radioactive waste from a nuclear power plant, if not contained, I feared it might unleash terrible damage. So I did what most Christians do: I lied a lot, both to myself and others."[2] In the name of peacekeeping, Scazzero tried to "get over" and guilt himself out of "negative" feelings about others' behavior, but he did it unsuccessfully, and ended up talking behind people's backs, making sarcastic or passive aggressive remarks, and/or withdrawing from relationships.

This type of false unity, of niceness, stunts the growth of our relationships and our self-awareness. Most of us were taught that we should not steer by our feelings, but our feelings are God-given warning lights that something is wrong under the hood. Many of us feel the sting of a careless remark by a treasured friend and don't ever tell them. We might feel frustration with a friend's chronic lateness or be hurt that they didn't treat an important event in our lives as a priority. And yet we don't say anything because we are afraid of appearing too sensitive. We actually wonder if we *are* too sensitive. We wish we were loving and patient enough to let more just roll off our backs.

Here's where Wendy's lesson comes in: we don't have to just get over our hurt feelings. Instead, we can find trust, restoration, intimacy, and freedom from bitterness by sharing our feelings in a respectful way. There is a greatness to giving our loved ones a chance to say, "Oh man! That is *not* what I meant." Or "I *totally* meant that, so we better talk about what is bothering *me*."

The One-Week Rule

If we're trying to be a wise person and not a fool, trying to decide to hold our peace or pursue peace through speaking up, I offer a guideline: the One-Week Rule. Often a friend says or does something that hurts, irritates, or angers us, but we're not ready to respond in the moment. This is wise: maybe we were crabby, hungry, or tired that day, so their comment rubbed us the wrong way. Or maybe it was their firstborn child's baby shower and it wouldn't have been appropriate to bring it up right then. When you feel a slight, a sting, or a slap, commit to yourself that you will say something to them about it within a week.

A few days' space from the incident can help us decide whether or not it's worth bringing to their attention. If it was a one-time comment, then maybe it isn't. If they were just stressed out or over-tired and said something out of character, we may decide to let it go, truly. Even if a friend did or said something that was in character, we don't need to point it out every time. For example, you have a friend who gives advice when you just felt like venting, and you've talked to her about it in the past. She might slip up now and then and jump in with a solution when she wasn't asked, but you can cut her some slack because you love her and she's trying.

But if you find that the feeling isn't fading, or worse yet, you are obsessing about it, pray for clarity. Try to avoid talking about it with a mutual friend, or triangulating, which can have lasting adverse effects in *every* relationship. If you must outwardly process, call someone from a different social circle.

Still upset? Then call your offending friend and talk about it. Maybe you are being oversensitive. Maybe some of your feelings are irrational. But the fact is, your friend is in a relationship with the real you, not the idealized you. The real you can get over some things, and some things you can't. Let your loved one see the real you, or the real you will find a way to show herself: in passive aggression, in retaliation, in leaving the friendship, or in blowing up at their second child's baby shower. Scazzero calls this delayed and violent reaction "leaking," which is kind of a gross term that makes me think of myself as a kitchen trash bag, something I really don't want to resemble.[3] But it's also a good way to remember how displeasing this trait is.

Over the course of a few days, ask yourself, *How did this incident make me feel?* Come up with a more specific word than *angry* or *sad.* Check out "The Feeling Wheel," created by psychologist Dr. Gloria Wilcox (you can find it easily in an internet search), which breaks down "sad" into twelve subsections that include "guilty," "lonely," and "bored." If you can tell someone that you feel dismissed, ignored, minimized or devalued, embarrassed or ashamed, attacked, or misunderstood, you've given them more insight and clarity.

Then consider, Does this feeling remind you of a time in your past? Remember, if you're hysterical, then it's probably historical. Ask yourself, *Was there another time in my life that I've felt this way, either in my childhood or my previous friendships? Is my reaction based on my personal history or is it a one-time feeling triggered by this incident in the present?* I've found that my emotional reactions are almost always in the first category.

After such introspection, you will have more to offer a friend than just, "When you said *x*, I was angry." You have a piece of your real self to offer them. Even if it turns out that you *are* being totally oversensitive, you now have a potential ally in your lifelong quest to be a less touchy person. Your friend pushed your buttons; now she has the opportunity to help you heal them. Don't misunderstand me. Your button is in your jurisdiction, but having someone in your life who cares and validates your feelings when that button gets pushed might really be helpful.

Sometimes the reason past hurts don't stay in the past is that they were never seen and validated; as children, most of us had a limited vocabulary to express our pain or understand the harm that was done to us. Now, as adults, we have the ability and opportunity to name these hurts with safe friends, which helps us heal. I learned how to do this in professional therapy sessions, but I practice it regularly with the amateur counselors who are my close girlfriends.

Here's an example, and I'm changing some names on this one:

Jane has been struggling with her health recently, and her doctor believes she has a number of food allergies and sensitivities that could be causing the problem. Jane and Kate go out to dinner with a group of friends. When Jane asks multiple questions about the menu, Kate says in front of the whole table, "Hurry up, picky. We're all starving!" Not the nicest thing anyone ever said, but not the worst thing either. Jane feels humiliated and hurt. It reminds her of when she was a child prone to stomachaches, and how her brothers, who could eat their weight in hamburgers and digest anything, would heckle her about it and fail to show her any compassion. After the dinner with friends, Jane lets a day or two pass, then she decides to give Kate a call. Instead of saying, "What you said at dinner was mean and I want you to apologize," she could instead say something like this:

"You probably don't realize this, but I've really been feeling sick lately, and my doctor thinks I need to try a specialized diet. I'm embarrassed about it: I don't like people to think of me as high-maintenance. My family always teased me about that, and it still bothers me when I think about it. Your comment hurt my feelings and reminded me of that. I really need your support in this new food thing I'm doing."

Unless Kate is an unsafe person or having a really, really bad day, her heart would be softened by that explanation. Now she can offer an apology for her thoughtless remark and feel trusted with the truth about her friend, rather than feeling like she's being accused of being a bad one. Next time she's out to dinner with Jane and a waiter is less than forthcoming with an ingredient list, Kate can support her and say, "Do what you gotta do, girl. I'm glad you're taking care of yourself."

You can see how this would be much more effective than if Jane had made a sharp comment right there at the table. She had some time to think it over and to handle the conflict in private. Jane now also has the benefit of a less-sensitive button due to Kate's understanding and support. Comments from others on the subject in the future are less likely to hurt.

The one-week rule is also important for this reason: it has an expiration date. Most people won't be angry that you waited a week to tell them they hurt your feelings. If you wait a month, or six months, or a year, I can guarantee they will. Like poor Harry in *When Harry Met Sally*, whose wife didn't tell him for weeks that she was divorcing him, and she even pretended to be happy at his birthday party first, they will not appreciate all the times they've spent with you when you pretended to be fine but were actually furious. Kate would think Jane was a little unreasonable for holding on to that offhand comment at a dinner party for six months. And frankly, Kate would be right.

When You're the One "In the Wrong"

The one-week rule also gives your friend time to have perspective about the situation and not be quite so defensive. Last week, someone honked at me, really long and hard, when I almost cut them off on the freeway. I was wrong, and what I did was dangerous (my husband jumped a foot in his seat when it happened), but in the moment, when I was being honked at, I felt more like throwing up an angry gesture than an apologetic wave. Because I was startled. And I was embarrassed because I had just been loudly reprimanded on a public street. If the same driver met me at Starbucks the next day and calmly said, "You know, you should maybe use your turn signal when you merge. Yesterday we both almost died fiery deaths on Interstate 5 due to your carelessness," I would have said, "You know, you're right, and I'm so sorry. Blessings to you, and may you be surrounded by safer drivers than me in the future" (if I'd already gotten my coffee, that is).

In *Safe People*, psychologists Cloud and Townsend define a quality of safe friends as those who are willing to admit their own faults. And I believe this is most important in the context of conflict. James 5:16 says, "Therefore, make it your habit to confess your sins to one another and to pray for one another, so that you may be healed" (ISV). Self-awareness and the ability to say we have issues is paramount to authentic living, and nowhere is that more important than when someone comes to you and says, "You hurt my feelings."

However, our immediate reactions are often denial, defensiveness, and self-justification. These reactions stem from shame, the result of perfectionism that says, "If I did something wrong, I *am* something wrong," a message we may have learned in our family of origin. This is described in *The 12 Steps and 12 Traditions Workbook of Codependents Anonymous* too: "In our childhoods, when we were vulnerable and admitted our imperfections, terrible things happened."[4] So when a friend says, "That comment made me feel minimized," we may be afraid to admit that we aren't perfect, that we are capable of insensitivity, because it feels to us like we're declaring, "I'm an insensitive *person*! I'm a *bad* friend!"

But accepting that we've hurt someone and showing compassion for them doesn't mean any of these things. It doesn't even mean that we were necessarily in the wrong for saying what we said. We may have pushed an emotional button without knowing it, which isn't really about us. But whatever the situation, no relationship has ever been improved by not being able to say, "I'm sorry I hurt you." You might fear that apologizing will put you in a position of weakness, that it will be used against you. But, girlfriend, let go of that worry; I've found that most people are much kinder than that. Healthy women are both charmed and disarmed by a sincere apology. They don't expect you to be perfect, and they will love you more for admitting that you aren't. So the question becomes, what do you expect of yourself? Do you think you're the only person in the world who always has to say the right thing in order to be considered a good friend? You don't. You can have grace like the rest of us.

Why "I'm Sorry" Is Essential

Most of us are initially defensive when we learn we have hurt someone. But I have begun to gauge the health of a friendship by how fast we are able to push past the situation, and own our stuff, in the context of conflict. As my girlfriends and I get healthier and come to trust each other more, the "I'm sorrys" happen more quickly. But just as the one-week rule gives us time to decide if it's necessary to mention a slight or injury, we also allow the one-week rule for the "offender" to be ready to come back with a sincere apology.

A sincere apology is key. Psychologist Harriet Lerner wrote,

A wholehearted apology means valuing the relationship, and accepting responsibility for our part without a hint of evasion, excuse-making, or blaming. Sometimes the process is less about insisting on justice and more about investing in the relationship and the other person's happiness. It's about accepting the people you love as they are . . . even when the other person's feelings seem exaggerated, or they can't see their own contribution to the problem. . . .

The need for apologies and repair is a singularly human one—both on the giving and receiving end. We're hard-wired to seek justice and fairness (however we see it), so the need to receive a sincere apology that's due is deeply felt. We're also imperfect human beings, prone to error and defensiveness, so the challenge of offering a heartfelt apology permeates almost every relationship. Tendering an apology, beyond the social gesture, can restore our sense of well-being and integrity when we sincerely feel we've done something wrong.[5]

Apologizing, confession of sin and wrongdoing, and restoring a relationship are central to our understanding of how God relates to us. Our relationships with God are based on repentance and grace. The book of 1 John says, "If we claim to be without sin, we deceive ourselves and the truth is not in us. If we confess our sins, he is faithful and just and will forgive us our sins and purify us from all unrighteousness. If we claim we have not sinned, we make him out to be a liar and his word is not in us" (1:8–10). Whether we call it our "issues" or we name it specifically—selfishness, thoughtlessness, being judgmental and critical, being unkind, coveting and competing—destructive sin is a part of our lives. So neither can we have sincere relationships with women without the practice of owning our issues being a regular part of our interactions. If we follow Jesus and understand the grace he has given us without condemnation, it will be easier to hear that we have wronged someone else and confess it freely without feeling shame.

In the first chapter we talked about self-awareness being key to authenticity; nowhere is this more important than when someone comes to us and says, "You hurt me." It gives us the opportunity to apologize, and personally, I never love anyone more—my husband, my kids, my friends—than when they apologize sincerely. It diffuses my anger and hurt like putting a pin back into a grenade. Never have I thought, *See? They admit they were wrong! Off with their heads!* If we regularly practice humility with each other, and grace is both given and received, we will build a level of comfort and confidence in the relationship, one that makes it unnecessary to even think in terms of right and wrong. Ultimately, we might make that our goal: to stop seeing conflict in black and white. Among imperfect people, hurt feelings and misunderstandings aren't always caused by one wrongdoer. Each of us brings our wounds, sensitivities, and sometimes clumsy communication to the table. When we love each other well, we seek to understand rather than just be understood, and then we can find the love we crave.

Lack of Repentance Is a Big Fat Red Flag

An essential question in our quest for healthy friendships is: What do you do when your friend has been in the wrong, you've told her about it and given her a week to process that she's hurt your feelings, and she still won't offer an apology or empathy? What do you do when you use all your introspective tools and "I feel" statements and she comes back with, "Oh yeah, well you are [blank, blank, *and* blank]!" My advice is to run screaming from the room and the relationship, locking the door on your way out.

Okay. Maybe not that. But guard your heart, my sister. As Proverbs 27:12 says, "The prudent see danger and take refuge, but the simple keep going and pay the penalty." I can't think of anything more emotionally dangerous than a friend who can't own her issues, *especially* when they have caused damage to your heart and soul. A friend that demands that you just "take her as she is" without allowing you to have any sensitivities or emotional needs is one who will hurt you again and again.

God has encouraged me to be brave many times in my life. He's sent me into a lot of places I wouldn't have gone without him pushing me. And yet, when I have come to him with a wounded heart from a chaotic or unsafe relationship and been willing to actually heed his instructions, never has he said, "Suck it up, girl. Get back in there and take it on the chin." Jesus said if someone strikes you on one cheek, turn and let them strike the other, but he also said not to give pearls to swine, and he told his disciples to shake the dust off their feet in the towns where they shared the gospel and the people were unrepentant. So there must be a place of limits and boundaries within friendships too. We are to love even our enemies and pray for those who persecute us, according to Jesus, but our friendships are the places where we choose to invest in relationships that will be *mutually* loving. We are called to love everyone, but not to trust everyone or create emotional transparency with everyone. We each need to be refueled within the context of loving relationships so that we can do the hard work God calls us to do in the big, cruel world.

Through his Spirit, Jesus has many times spoken his love, grace, and protection over me in relationships. He has given me permission to authentically expose hurt feelings to friends and then, when they can't own their part in the problem, to step back for a season or to leave the relationship altogether. He has gifted me with women who see me—issues and all—and don't tell me that there must be something wrong with *me* if I'm not perfectly happy with *them*. They are my soft places to land, where my thoughts, feelings, and insecurities are understood. Through this grace, I have—amazingly—been made stronger and more secure. By being loved by worthy friends, I have become more of a friend worth having.

Sisters, I'm with you in the trenches of conflict and hurt feelings in friendships. Prayer is a key way I've sought wisdom and healing because God always listens and he always answers in some way. Over the years, when I've encountered conflict, I've prayed something like this:

> Lord, you give wisdom to all without finding fault. Search me and know my anxious thoughts. Give me insight into my own feelings, and help me to distinguish whose "issue" [friend's name] and I are dealing with right now. Please help me discern if I should speak up or stay silent about the hurt I'm feeling. And show me what needs fixing on my side of the street. Give us a spirit of compassion and love for one another. In Jesus' name, amen.

You can do this, sisters. In a world where all our friends have issues, conflict is to be expected, and learning to navigate it will strengthen your bonds. God already knows our struggles, and he is ready to help us work through them.

Part 2

ENCOURAGEMENT

You are hanging on by a very thin thread and I dig that about you!

—ROD TIDWELL IN *JERRY MAGUIRE*

Let us hold unswervingly to the hope we profess, for he who promised is faithful. And let us consider how we may spur one another on toward love and good deeds, not giving up meeting together, as some are in the habit of doing, but encouraging one another—and all the more as you see the Day approaching.

—HEBREWS 10:23–25

Chapter 5

IN LIEU OF FLOWERS, PLEASE SEND EMOJIS

Daily Encouragement in Its Many Beautiful Forms

I need you to text me every thirty seconds saying that everything is gonna be okay.

—LESLIE KNOPE IN *PARKS AND RECREATION*

A tragic loss occurred in my life last summer. Due to a necessary reboot of my iPhone, which cleared it of everything but my contacts, all my text messages were erased.

When I thought of the wisdom, encouragement, and Pinterest images that were lost, I could have wept. In this age of busyness and disconnection, with my friends working away in their homes and offices on opposite sides of our gridlocked county, the texts from my tribe are what sometimes get me through the day.

I realized the importance of these brief [life] lines when my phone was dead, and my first instinct was to text to a friend: "Argh! Phone went black! Must spend hours at Apple store to remedy situation."

No doubt, this message would have been responded to with: "Oh no! Hang in there, darling. Deep breaths."

And it would have been enormously helpful.

Without this little friendly contact, I felt like adulting just got a lot tougher. (My kids were home for the summer! I didn't sign them up for camps! I was outnumbered!) Suddenly, there was no buffer between me and the cruel world of modern inconveniences, emotional meltdowns (mine and the kids'), and mystifying situations (*Should I call that coach who was rude to my daughter? Do you think this purse is "me"?*).

So not only did I endure the cruel purgatory of the Apple store without help or distraction, but I lost at least two weeks' history of love through text.

So, so much did I lose that I made a bid through my social media accounts when I was back online: "I'm in mourning for the loss of all my text messages. If you have any compassion for my situation, in lieu of flowers, please send emojis." Messages with emojis poured in. It was a good day.

By the way, if *you* would ever like to text me in the future, here's what I would appreciate:

- For empathy, I like the stressed face, the wailing face, the green nauseous face.
- To help me keep from taking myself too seriously, I find the wink with the tongue out to be helpful.
- Please laugh at my jokes with the LOL crying emoji.

- If I have good news, celebrate by sending me the girl doing a handstand or the salsa dancer.
- And finally, just show me you love me. Heart-eye emoji and kissing emoji will do the trick. One of my friends also sends rainbows, hedgehogs, and bacon.

Even more important than emojis, and harder to replace, were all the pieces of advice, scriptures, and quotations I'd received to keep my heart healthy and my head above water. The blessing of losing those texts was realizing how precious they were to me. And the good news is, they will keep on coming.

Case in point: as soon as my iPhone was restored, my friend Sophie and I resumed our regular mutual mentoring via text. I, a working mother of two, she a wedding coordinator and dog mama of two, can count on one another to keep our hearts pointed in the right direction and to engage in healthy behaviors. Exhibit A:

Me: Bad day. Want beer.

Sophie: Bad day for me too. I got a speeding ticket and my job is making me feel like people are mad at me. We don't need beer. We can take a bath.

Me: Or go to the gym.

Sophie: Or watch Netflix.

Me: Nobody is mad at you. Brides are crazy and you are saving their white-dressed booties every day even if they don't know it.

Sophie: Thank you.

[Time passes.]

Me: I went to Zumba.

Sophie: Do you still want beer?

Me: No. Now I want coconut water and cashews.

Sophie: [high five emoji]

I see in those lines so many ways in which Sophie and I know each other's heart goals and struggles. She knows that I quit drinking alcohol in order to focus on some specific aspects of my spiritual life. I know that she is a recovering workaholic and people pleaser that needs to be reminded that she is great at her job but not defined by it. We both need to be reminded to eat—not only healthy food, but *any* food (we are both stress non-eaters). Many of our conversations are even deeper: about overcoming codependency, a relational dysfunction we both share in which we allow people's opinions of us to outweigh God's. Left unchecked it's a subtle, complex, debilitating dysfunction, and sometimes it takes one codependent to speak into the life of another.

Encouragement According to Our Needs

The great gift of authenticity in our relationships with other women is that it leads to this kind of authentic encouragement. Ephesians 4:29 calls this "building others up according to their needs." If you don't know someone well, how can you know what will encourage them?

The New Testament uses the Greek word for encouragement *parakaleo* 108 times. It means "to call to one's side, call for, or summon," and also "to address, speak to by way of exhortation, entreaty, comfort, instruction." *Parakaleo* also has the meaning "to console, comfort, and strengthen."[1] Paul is usually the one writing encouragement to the churches and exhortation to encourage others: encouragement to walk in faith, to follow God's holy instructions, to love one another, and to be confident in our identity in Christ as loved children who were made for a purpose.

The English definitions of *encourage* closest to *parakaleo* are

1. To receive consolation, be comforted
2. To strengthen
3. Exhorting and comforting
4. To instruct, teach

In my text stream with Sophie, I see all aspects of encouragement: our attempts to teach, inspire, console, and strengthen one another. We persuade each other of the truths we have learned about ourselves and each other. When one of us has slipped into believing lies about our unworthiness, we console the other. We empower each other to make good choices. We remind each other of the great hope that God is remaking us and we get to participate in that process. And that the process of becoming the best version of ourselves is worth it.

When we understand what encouragement really means, we realize that there's no such thing as one-size-fits-all encouragement: the words of affirmation and encouragement we each need are as specific as the type of jeans we wear. Where a meek friend may need to be told to speak up and defend herself or her children, the one who's working on self-control and gentleness may need to be affirmed when she chooses to stand down. One might need to be cheered when she makes it to the gym, and another might need to be applauded when she relaxes and just eats a cupcake already because eating dessert would be a sign that she is being released from the stronghold of body obsession.

Listen First, Encourage Second

We often think of encouragement as being about what we say. But the first step of being an encouraging friend is listening. At this, I often fail. When I'm driving to meet a friend for coffee, on the way I am always thinking of all the things I'm excited to tell her rather than the questions I want to ask. But asking and listening is paramount. Everyone needs to be listened to. They need it more than they need advice or an encouraging word. A respected marriage and family therapist in my church says his clients come and talk for forty-five minutes, and often he does no more than repeat back to them what he hears them say. At the end of the session, they thank him for the good advice even though he didn't give any.

I have a sinful tendency, maybe you can relate, in that I want to be seen as someone who has good advice and wisdom to offer, which is more about me feeling good than about making other people feel good. Sometimes I'm so quick to encourage that I don't actually hear what my friends need. I think of Philippians 2:3–4: "Do nothing out of selfish ambition or vain conceit. Rather, in humility value others above yourselves, not looking to your own interests but each of you to the interests of the others." When I sit still and listen to my friends, I'm amazed at the miracle that happens in my self-obsessed heart. I begin to take a very sincere interest in their interests. I begin to see them a little more as God sees them, fully loved, precious, and made for a purpose. And then, I begin to offer encouragement that is more than situational: it's spiritual, and I speak into them the personal promises of God and speak against the lies they believe about themselves.

One of the sweetest pictures of female friendship in Scripture is brief but profound, and it is found in the gospel of Luke. When Mary hears from God that she will carry and deliver the Messiah, she hurries to the house of her cousin Elizabeth. On the way I imagine that Mary has already begun to be flooded with doubts about what God said to her. *Really? Am I really the one to carry the Messiah? Is this an honor or a punishment? What is going to happen*

74

to me and Joseph? Who will believe me? Won't this bring me cursing from the people rather than honor?

But the moment she walks into her cousin's house, Elizabeth says, in a loud voice, "Blessed is she who has believed that the Lord would fulfill his promises to her!" (Luke 1:45).

I imagine that is exactly what Mary needed to hear, and it's what we each need to hear every day in small, large, and extremely specific ways.

I really desire to build my friends up in the way they most need, and listening to them helps. But there's someone else I need to listen to even more: the Holy Spirit. Elizabeth seems totally in tune with the Lord when Mary shows up at her house, and we too should desire this connection with him if we want to love and encourage our friends well. I discuss this at length in the final chapter—and please feel free to skip ahead. If your friend has an ongoing issue and you desire to build her up, first, pray and ask God to speak to you about what she truly needs to hear, and for his timing to guide your words. Through prayer for one another, you may be able to see God's will in these situations:

- The friend who is overcoming shame from her past needs to be encouraged that God has removed all her sins.
- The friend who struggles with her value as related to body image (whether she works out obsessively or puts it off out of guilt) needs to be cheered that her soul is God's masterpiece, and that her body is merely a tent (Eph. 2:10; 2 Cor. 5:1).
- The friend who doubts her own thoughts and intellect, who cowers from speaking the truth when the truth needs to be spoken, needs to be reminded that she has not been given a spirit of fear, "but of power, and of love, and of a sound mind" (2 Tim. 1:7 KJV).

- The friend who struggles with depression, including guilt over struggling with depression, needs to be reminded of David, Elijah, the authors of Lamentations, and all the other men and women of faith who authentically poured out their struggling hearts to God and were loved and accepted.
- The friend who struggles with feeling purposeless needs to be reminded that God has prepared good things for her to do (also Eph. 2:10) and gifted her with talents that the body of Christ needs (1 Cor. 12).
- But first, each of these women needs to be allowed to talk it all out.

What would each of our lives be like if we had one or two special women who listened to us, knew us, and spoke affirmation into our lives? I think fewer of us would need therapy. And the husbands of those of us who are married wouldn't even know who to thank for how much happier their wives seem.

Advice and Encouragement: An Important Distinction

In the church, I find that women are great encouragers—*if* the encouragement is allowed to come in the form of advice. A new mom says she is having trouble sleeping, and we bombard her with suggestions for herbal remedies, melatonin supplements, baby sleep-training books, relaxing bedtime yoga routines, and prayer rituals that will help. In more serious scenarios, such as a woman having a real come-to-Jesus moment, when she's confronting and sincerely mourning her own sin, we might come to her rescue with "encouraging" scriptures about her identity in Christ when her identity is not the issue at the moment: her issue is one of healing and needing to change behaviors.

We mean well. We really do. But sometimes, sitting in our cabin at a women's retreat or around the table at Bible study, we don't recognize how uncomfortable we are with the pain of the woman across from us, so we give advice or encouragement to put her—and us—out of misery as quickly as possible. Or sometimes, we believe we know what's best for others when we really don't know them very well at all.

It's probably no surprise to you, reader, that my least favorite verse in all of Scripture is "Everyone should be quick to listen [and] slow to speak" (James 1:19). As a woman of many, many words, it's a hard one to follow. But heed this advice, fellow loving, outspoken women who are ready to cheer others on to greatness. The kind of greatness you have achieved might not be the greatness the women in your Bible study or play group are working toward. Some of the words and even scriptures we might use to encourage someone can end up putting them in bondage rather than setting them free if we offer it in ignorance of their issues—their circumstances, history, strongholds, and heartbreaks. Consider the harm of advising a woman to be patient and long-suffering in her marriage, for example, when her husband has been physically abusive to her and her children.

I'm hyper aware of how misplaced one-size-fits-all encouragement can lead to enslavement. When I speak to large groups of women, I know that, in every audience, there is a Perfectionist who is already getting an A in life but is killing herself trying to get an A-plus. For her, I'm careful not to add to her to-do list by telling her to buy only organic produce, or to make her feel too guilty about checking her text messages occasionally at her son's softball game. Also in the audience is the Religious Legalist, a subsect of the Perfectionist; for her, I don't ever set a quota on how much time she should pray, how much Scripture she should know by heart, or how many items should be on her gratitude list before she's allowed to bring her laments to the Lord. For the People Pleaser, I make sure not to use language that makes her feel she has someone to please other than God, or that making people happy is her job. (For the record, loving people and making them happy is not the same thing.)

I'm sensitive to each of these types of women because they are types I used to be. I get aggravated when other teachers don't do the same (and I confess my pride before God right now). But I recently attended a conference for young mothers, and one of the keynote speakers spent thirty minutes teaching on being more self-sacrificing. I wanted to get up on stage and scream: "These are mothers of infants who are also *volunteering* their time to help other mothers! Don't tell them to sacrifice more! Tell them how pleased God is with what they are sacrificing already!"

I can't possibly know the specific needs of every woman I teach, but I can seek to know and understand the women with whom I'm friends, those who have asked me to come alongside them and build them up. I can know their issues: the struggles they have, the lies they believe, the goals they've set. And armed with this knowledge, I can cheer them on toward love and good deeds and not toward further bondage. Especially if I pray for God's timing. Will you join me?

- I won't encourage selflessness in a friend who is being taken advantage of by an abusive spouse, boss, or parent.
- I won't encourage more hard work and diligence in a friend who has burned herself out.
- I won't tell a friend who has just confronted childhood sexual abuse to move right into forgiveness.
- I won't tell a friend who is being pressured by an enmeshed church body to put unity above her own God-given instincts.

If You Need Something, Say Something

One final word for this chapter: if you need encouragement, ask for it. The general rule of desire is that we are responsible for making our desires known. This is easier if you are convinced of this truth: God is a good Father who wants to meet your desire for encouragement. Consider the beautiful treasure in the story of Mary and Elizabeth: if anyone should have felt alone, it was Mary who was facing a miraculous, angel-announced, scandal-inducing pregnancy. And yet God provided a cousin, friend, and mentor in Elizabeth, who was also facing a miraculous, angel-announced, scandal-inducing pregnancy. But Mary had to "get ready and hurry to the house of Elizabeth" (Luke 1:39) to find the encouragement God had provided for her.

Go and do likewise. Because if God can find someone for Mary, he surely has someone to encourage you. Tell people what you want for your birthday. Ask for a hug. When you feel down, discouraged, or in need of someone to tell you to finish the project you started—or maybe even remind you why you started it in the first place—call a friend and ask. When you're unsure if God will fulfill his promises to you after all, ask a friend to remind you of his faithfulness. If you've been authentic with her in the past, she'll know what kind of encouragement you need. In words, in text, in emojis. Whatever.

Chapter 6

SABBATICAL SISTERS AND SELF-CARE

Encouraging Our Besties to Take a Break

You get warning signs, and then you realize that you are not
a tank, as [his wife] Ali says. Edge has this thing that he says
about me, that I look upon my body as an inconvenience.

—BONO, *THE ROLLING STONE* INTERVIEW, JANUARY 2018

Part of my bond with my uber-intelligent, eminently sensible friend Elizabeth is our mutual love of the band U2, and particularly its front man, Bono. Both of us have held a torch for him since *Joshua Tree* was released in 1987 (I was in the fourth grade; Elizabeth was in high school. I'm younger. I win.). We love his music, the fact that he has somehow combined biblical faith and rock and roll (he *does* use the f-word in interviews, I acknowledge), and that he also has become an activist for the extreme poor throughout the world. Elizabeth says one of the things she most looks forward to in heaven is talking theology with Bono.

Another thing Elizabeth and I have in common is our penchant for volunteerism. We met as volunteer MOPS leaders, and we both served long terms. I remember going to her house a year after she "retired" and finding her drinking coffee out of a mug that said, "Stop me before I volunteer again!" And yet Elizabeth continued to serve her community as an art docent, a small-group Bible study leader, a PTA member, a fund-raiser, and the director of her children's school play, basically bringing salt and light to the world. We are both what I would call compulsive volunteers, tending to love others beyond what our bodies, brains, and calendars can comfortably withstand.

So when I recently read *The Rolling Stone* interview of Bono, just after the band released the *Songs of Experience* album, I had to send the quote above about Bono treating his body as an inconvenience to my friend. And she wrote back: "A jar of clay . . ."

I love Elizabeth.

Our culture does not affirm the truth of Scripture Elizabeth is referencing—that we have treasure in our frail bodies, which are jars of clay, as we carry the love of God and message of Christ (2 Cor. 4:7–9). On the contrary, culture asserts that our job is to turn our bodies into tanks that never age, that can keep on going no matter what life throws at them. Until after five o'clock. When we binge-watch TV and drink alcohol to escape. American culture values busyness, achievement, earning, and accumulating.

The church does not exactly offer an alternative to this way of thinking. Though self-care is currently a buzzword in both Christian and secular culture, few people actually practice it. Many of us who are Christians believe that if we serve in the Holy Spirit, we will live out the verse, "run and not grow weary, walk and never be faint" (Isa. 40:31). In fact, churches tend to systematically encourage us when we overextend. A church staff might be so passionate about God's work and so desperate for help that they do not discourage an avid volunteer. I'm part of a beautiful megachurch in Southern California, and there are so many opportunities to serve, attend Bible study, and participate in programs that I have to say no to good things all the time. That used to be really, really hard for me.

Can Someone Please Tell Me It's Okay to Stop?

Enter my long-term, encouraging relationship with my friend Gina. Gina and I also met in MOPS, which at our church is a kind of training ground for young female leaders, a place we can serve, grow, and use our gifts during the era when we are sleep deprived and have spit-up on our shoulders. Gina and I each led a group of more than one hundred young moms for several years. We each then took on the role of "Core Moms Coordinator," a volunteer position that oversaw multiple young mothers' ministries. I went first, then left the job halfway through what was supposed to be a two-year term. Gina followed me; then she also left the job after only one year.

After a decade of volunteer service in women's ministry, Gina and I both found ourselves in the same place: burned out, burdened with guilt over getting out "early," and wondering what the heck we were going to do with ourselves. We were both sure we had heard God's voice call us to a new season outside of a formal leadership position in the church. But what would we even tell people we *were* now? We decided to call ourselves the Sabbatical Sisters, and it comforted us to have a name, though we used it only with each other and our husbands.

A professional's sabbatical is a period of paid leave granted to a university teacher or other worker for study or travel, traditionally one year for every seven years worked. Teachers will be better equipped to teach if they are given a break every seven years to actually experience life, so the thinking goes. Gina and I had had a decade of *unpaid* work, so we figured we could have a year of unpaid rest too. God had said so.

The next two years in our lives produced much fruit—and change. Gina pulled all four of her kids out of public school and began homeschooling. I know, it doesn't sound like rest, but for Gina's unique family, stepping outside the paradigm of mainstream public education produced a kind of peace they had not before known. Then God took Gina to the desert, both literally and figuratively. Their family moved out of high-priced Coastal Orange County to a more affordable, slower paced inland community. Gina left her church, her friends (poor me!), and many sources of her identity.

Meanwhile, I took the advice of my friend and author Barb Egbert and slowed *way* down to make emotional space for my two daughters, who were six and ten at the time. My ten-year-old especially needed to see that Mama had space to talk to her; she's a deep-thinking, intelligent, introverted kid who needs time to talk when she feels like it. I spent a lot of time sitting in my kitchen being available, ready to receive her confidences and bursts of silliness.

Both Gina and I struggled deeply with issues of identity in those two years, and without each other, we would have also really struggled with loneliness. The odd thing we both found within our hearts was how guilty we felt—a guilt that bordered on depression—for not pushing ourselves so hard. We struggled with pride in dark moments: Why did so many women seem to be able to do it all and have it all while our minds, bodies, and spirits had "given out" and made us quit? If it weren't for the conviction that God had led us out of formal ministry (I believed he had told me, "Go where I send thee," and I knew it wasn't to leadership in my home church), we probably wouldn't have made it. But God used that time and our friendship to teach us about how much he desires us to have rest, balance, and margin in our lives. How much he wants us to be able to give out of a full cup and not an empty one. And how much value we have simply because we are his, humble jars of clay though we are. We learned in those two years to trust in God and not in the world's version of success.

Our sabbaticals were fruitful. Gina is now part of an amazing prayer ministry at her desert church, has found her stride as a homeschooling mother, and has supported her husband through a stressful but lucrative career change. As for me, my daughter is now fifteen, and I'm reaping the benefits of living with so much margin in my life during that formative preteen stage of her life. Now here I go with daughter number two, aged eleven.

Meanwhile, in those two years I also wrote a book about what it means for women of faith to live according to what we love and value rather than according to what culture says we need to accomplish. I taught it as a Bible study to two separate groups of friends. I also wrote talks for MOPS groups and slowly started a speaking ministry to other moms. All of those experiences led to the book you're reading now. And I couldn't have done it without my Sabbatical Sister.

In a culture that tells us we are what we produce, friends that affirm our right to say no, rest, and listen to God's leading are more precious than one thousand Instagram followers.

Be Sick and Take a Sabbath

One of my weirdest issues is that I really need someone to tell me it's okay to be sick. Being sick makes me feel like a loser. I'm like Monica on *Friends*, trying to seduce Chandler with Vicks VapoRub to prove she's too tough to have a cold. I also struggle with migraines. They hit me about once every four to six weeks, and if I don't take medicine and go straight to a dark room, they last twice as long. I despise being taken out like that; it's not even the excruciating pain that bothers me. It's that I can't get anything *done*! My body is such an *inconvenience*.

I'm so weird about this that sometimes I have to post on Facebook that I don't feel well, just so someone in the universe will know, sympathize, and tell me to go to bed. (I don't want to call anyone. I feel too sick.) I've posted:

"Head hurts. Sore throat. [facemask emoji]."

This experiment has really paid off. No one has ever posted a comment that says, "Suck it up and keep going!" or "Go to the grocery store anyway. Infect everyone else!" Instead, my girlfriends say things like, "Take care of yourself," "Watch a movie," "Drink tea and sleep," or even, "Can I pick up the kids at school for you?"

And I've decided nothing makes me feel so loved as someone who tells me it's okay to take care of myself, whether I'm sick, sad, exhausted, hormonal, or otherwise indisposed.

I've been conditioned to be averse to self-care in general, and I'm working to reprogram myself. I used to be racked with guilt if I bought myself a sandwich while out running errands, so instead I'd go home hypoglycemic, cranky, and spent after a day of taking care of business for my family. I've discovered I'm not alone in this issue. Personally, almost all of us would say to our friends, "It's okay to take care of *you*," but almost every woman I run around with has a hard time telling that to herself.

Among women of the Christian faith, the Sabbath is probably the least-followed commandment of the ten (followed closely by "do not covet," which we'll talk about in the next chapter). The breaking of it is connected to the first commandment, which is "Have no other gods before the one true God." *I* am not *him*. And even *he* took a break to enjoy himself. What does it say about my faith if I don't believe I'm worth a sandwich and a nap?

Rest. Be refreshed. The term *sabbatical* comes from the root word *sabbath*, and the every-seven-years principle comes from God's command to the Israelites to let the fields lie fallow in the seventh year. We push against this boundary. We have too much pride to slow down. Or maybe we are afraid we aren't worthy of care. Either way, we are failing to honor God and the way he made us. Jesus said, "The Sabbath was made for man, not man for the Sabbath." Which means God won't get mad at you if you pick grain or throw in a load of laundry on Sunday, but he gives you permission and encouragement to wait until Monday to do it.

Sayings for Sabbatical Sisters

I often see T-shirts and Pinterest posts that say, "You've got this, girl." And it's nice encouragement. Really. But frankly, just as often, I would be more encouraged by someone saying to me, "You *don't* got this, girl. But I'm praying for you. God will show up for you. First, take a nap if you need one." But that doesn't fit on a T-shirt.

Because the battle for rest and self-care is real and spiritual, get yourself some Sabbatical Sisters: co-warriors against the culture of do more, be more. Encourage one another in this special way. A practical way to do this is to remind one another of all a woman does every day—all the demands placed on her by her work, her spouse, her friends, her parents, her family. We sometimes forget the value of our work and we need to be reminded that we've done a lot; we've done enough.

Continuing to encourage each other in this way is part of how God—who is willing that we should have abundant life in him—releases us from this subtle stronghold, this two-sided coin of pride and unworthiness.

Speak these truths over one another:

- You are God's loved child, just as you are.
- You don't have to be perfect.
- You don't have to be all things to all people.
- It's okay to say no.
- I appreciate you.
- When you're sick, take a sick day.
- When you're tired, take a nap.
- When you're hungry, buy a sandwich.
- When you're sad, go ahead and cry.
- If you're burned out, miss just this one meeting/Bible study/ work function/school function.
- God will provide; it's not all up to you.
- Take your meds.
- Take your vitamins.
- There's enough good in good enough.
- Don't volunteer for one. More. Thing.
- You are a treasure in a jar of clay.

Chapter 7

TWO SUPERHEROES AND NO SIDEKICK

Overcoming Competition, Comparison, and Codependency

I'm so jealous. That's it. I've got to get some dumb, ugly
friends.

—LANE IN *GILMORE GIRLS*

My first "real" writing gig was a bimonthly column for my college
newspaper, *The Mustang Daily.* I wrote about important subjects,
such as adventures in my 1988 Mazda 323 hatchback named Melvin
the Disco Biscuit; why guys should stay out of the TV lounge in
the student union during the *Days of Our Lives* hour; and my daily
conflict with my archnemesis, Cranky Bus Driver Lady. In one
week's column, I wrote under the persona of Happy College Student
Girl, and my heroic goal was to get the bus driver to say, "Good
morning." She never would do it. She barely nodded. One day she
said, "Don't eat that bagel on my bus."

As I look back over my life, I realize that I have always had what I consider to be a nemesis, if only in a humorous sense. There's consistently been someone I've thought of as standing *against* everything I stand *for*: community, whimsy, honesty, and letting go of perfectionism. It somehow has seemed to give my life a little more interest to have a Newman to my Seinfeld, a Mr. Heckles to my Rachel and Monica, a Slugworth to my Willy Wonka.

One nemesis I had more recently was a woman I referred to as the Non-Smiler. I passed her every day on the sidewalk outside my daughters' school, and she refused to return my "good mornings" or smiles. In a moment in which I was so *not* acting like Jesus, I told another mom about it, and together we imagined organizing a flash mob to sing "Good Morning" à la Debbie Reynolds in *Singin' in the Rain* to her as she walked down the sidewalk. The plan never came to fruition. And thank God, because the Non-Smiler nemesis turned out to be the mother of one of my daughter's good friends. When we were finally thrown together in a play-date situation, she turned out to be not grumpy or nemesis-worthy at all, but instead an intelligent person, a thoughtful mother, a serious thinker, and a hard worker. In other words, a person I really like. She's just not that smiley to strangers.

Other "enemies" have included gossips, Alpha Moms who boss committees and yell at soccer referees, and neighbors who write nasty letters to the homeowners' association board. And it occurred to me that in my own imagination, in which I wear a cape and am the good-if-slightly-ridiculous-and-disorganized heroine, that I am not quite as nice as I think I am. I create the hero-vs-nemesis story line because being cast as the hero in my own story allows me to compare myself to others and come out on top. It allows me to be judgmental and competitive and see my life, my choices, and my ways of being as better than others'. And unchecked, this tendency toward comparison and competition would not lead me to a happy ending. No one wins in a community where women are striving to look better and feel superior to those around them. If we ever do make it to the top this way, we'll likely find the old adage to be true: it's lonely up there.

Not-So-Friendly Competition

These stories about my nemeses are included in a book about female friendship because I believe we don't just struggle with competing with our archenemies. We struggle with competing with our friends because competition between women is so pervasive in our culture. *The Bachelor* is in its twenty-second season, and if that doesn't prove that women like to judge each other, I don't know what will. In addition to its attraction as romantic escapism, women love reality shows like *The Bachelor* because it allows us to be gossipy about other women without feeling guilty; once they're on television, they're fair game.

For these reasons I believe women who truly have an affection for one another's well-being will change the world and win women to Christ. They will stand out like bright lights in our competitive culture. Jesus said, "By this all the world will know that you are my disciples, if you love one another." And Paul said, "Love is not proud and does not boast." In other words, love does not compete. Love says, "I love how God made you. Go be the best version of yourself." But often, our lack of confidence in the way God made *us* makes it hard for us to celebrate how God made *others*.

Here's an example of how it often goes down among women: my daughter Olivia was in Girl Scouts for five years, and I'm a little too disorganized and rebellious to be a particularly good mother to a Girl Scout with all its correct badge-placement and permission-slip signing. But when themed snacks are involved, I have a talent to contribute. One year on St. Patrick's Day, I made marshmallow treats with Lucky Charms instead of Rice Krispies and fruit skewers in a rainbow pattern. When I showed up for the meeting with my tray, none of the moms said, "How cute! How fun! Thanks for doing this for our daughters!" Instead a couple of them said, "Man, you're making us all look bad."

Even though they were joking (I think), I walked away feeling kind of depressed at the state of womanhood. Look, I'm lousy at permission slips. And the year I tried to be the Girl Scout troop's Cookie Manager, I screwed up the inventory in the Excel spreadsheet so badly that my husband had to come home from work and rescue me the day it was due. But I can make a rainbow fruit skewer. Can someone please celebrate that with me?

At the same time, I understand. I know I've made the same kinds of comments to other women who are good at things I struggle with (like those who always remember the permission slips, or look good in tight, patterned workout pants). But I'm working on it, sisters. Will you join me? Because even these casual remarks of comparison reinforce the lie that we are rivals rather than running mates in the race to live out our purpose.

Confidence and Competition

Competition and comparison between women can keep us from making friends in the first place. When we haven't dealt with our own feelings of unworthiness, when we aren't secure in who God made us to be and what we have to offer the world, it will be very hard to be attracted to other people. Women who possess qualities we wish we had will instead become repellent to us.

A woman who is too stylish, too fit, too organized, too smart, too happy, too spiritual, too in love with her boyfriend or husband, too successful, too good a cook or housekeeper, or has her makeup too professionally applied might make us want to run the other way. Most of us would like to be stylish, organized, smart, fit, happy, in love, and "successful" at work and home. Every woman's magazine we buy is trying to help us achieve these intangibles. But someone who has attained them throws into sharp relief the ones we are lacking.

Our lack of confidence is one cause of competition. I've noticed another subtle source. Some women raised in the church may have received the message that focusing on our good qualities will make us puffed up and prideful. Actually, it doesn't just happen in church. A very popular song a few years back praised a girl for being insecure, saying, "You don't know you're beautiful. And that's what makes you beautiful." Excuse me, what? Being unable to appreciate your good qualities or even to recognize them—external beauty, intelligence, talent, whatever—is not more spiritual than recognizing that you are a precious, purposeful, miracle of God. Some of us noticed that our good qualities made others feel badly, so we learned to hide our light under a bushel, to cease to be the full expression of who we are, and then to resent those who let their light shine freely.

As a Christian I believe what Jesus taught: that he came to bring us abundant life because he loves us. He also taught that we have a spiritual enemy who hates us and wants to undermine God's love and our purpose. The enemy will try to get us at every turn: making us afraid of our weakness and afraid of our power. I believe we *must* outwit him and encourage each other to shine bright so that we can live out the truth: we are precious and made for a purpose.

I Need Some Dumb, Ugly Friends

God instructed us not to covet in the Ten Commandments because coveting damages relationships. You cannot be authentic and encouraging with someone whose husband or home you wish was yours. But don't be too hard on yourselves, sisters. We are all guilty of the sin of envy at some point. What we don't have almost always seems like the best thing. Envy is so hard to conquer that we might be tempted to throw up our hands as *Gilmore Girls* character Lane did and say, "That's it, I have to get some dumb, ugly friends!" But that doesn't seem like a very practical or spiritual solution. Instead, we have to get real about our feelings of envy and learn how to deal with them, not just deny them or stuff them down.

I love the insightful and proactive way Cloud and Townsend approach the problem of envy in *Boundaries:*

> The problem with envy is that it focuses outside our boundaries, onto others. If we are focusing on what others have or have accomplished, we are neglecting our responsibilities and will ultimately have an empty heart. Look at the difference in Galatians 6:4: "Each one should test his own actions. Then he can take pride in himself, without comparing himself to somebody else. . . ."
>
> Your envy should always be a sign to you that you are lacking something. At that moment, you should ask God to help you understand what you resent, why you do not have whatever you are envying, and whether you truly desire it. Ask him to show you what you need to do to get there, or to give up the desire.[1]

In twelve-step Codependents Anonymous recovery, participants are encouraged to work with a sponsor and to ask someone who has qualities you'd like to have in yourself. If the person agrees to sponsor you, she will share with you the hard steps she took to get where she is today. Then you get to decide if you're going to follow those same steps or not.

What if making friends functioned the same way? Once we've acknowledged honestly that we see something in another woman that we want, what if we asked her to be our friend, and if she agrees, what if we asked her to share the path that she took to gain the skills or character quality we admire? What if we allowed ourselves to be drawn in by her power, peace, and ability to enjoy life; her beauty (inner and outer); and her ability to use her gifts to glorify God and live in victory? What if her goodness and worthiness made her attractive rather than threatening to us? What if we were not her competitors, but asked her to teach and encourage us? Instead of being repelled by her awesomeness and our own insecurity, what if we had the courage to work it out in relationship with her?

I have done this in my own life. For years I was envious of Jen's body. She's a buff babe. I never allowed my envy to become full-fledged resentment, but I did not enjoy standing next to her in my bathing suit. I began to observe why Jen was so comfortable in hers: she was very self-disciplined about exercise and healthy food choices. I, on the other hand, was very averse to sweating and very pro-donut. When I turned thirty-five, I made a decision: I would allow Jen to inspire and encourage me and I joined a gym. Five years later, I'm in much better shape than I was and I feel a lot better about my body, even if I'm not exactly a candidate for a before-and-after ad. Jen taught me a lot about how to effectively exercise to build muscle and protect bone mass. And to this day, my best workouts are our long walks together. Then we have brunch, and she gets the side salad while I get the potatoes. (I know what I like to eat and am not willing to make *that* much of a sacrifice.)

It's a tougher boat to row if what you envy in a friend is something that you will never be able to attain, such as their height or hair color or their spiritual gifts. The sagest advice I have in that case is to lean into the Lord. In 1 Corinthians, Paul talks about our spiritual gifts in terms of the human body: some of us are hands, and some of us are eyes or feet. Some of the parts of the body that might seem unpresentable are treated with special modesty. Our faith is really challenged in this: Do we really believe what 1 Corinthians 12:22 says, that those parts of the body that seem to be weaker are actually indispensable? Frankly, I really don't want to be a foot, an elbow, or something that needs to be covered up—special modesty or not. I'd much rather be an eye, or a right hand with a good manicure.

We do not all have equal gifts in the sight of the world, which honors some talents (such as those that come with money, fame, or more "likes" on Instagram) more than others, but we do have equal worth in the sight of God. For the health of my heart and relationships, I strive to accept this in faith: "God has put the body together, giving greater honor to the parts that lacked it, so that there should be no division in the body, but that its parts should have equal concern for each other. . . . If one part is honored, every part rejoices with it" (1 Cor. 12:24–26). When we fully embrace our own value in God's sight, we will truly be loving, noncompetitive friends.

Much more significant than Jen's contribution to my muscle mass is this: Jen is an extremely loyal encourager of my ministry. She has believed with me that God placed a writing and teaching calling on my life, and she has supported me through endless discussions, praying for me faithfully and purchasing cross-country airline tickets so she could come along when I got my first big gig. Once there, she prayed for me before I went onstage and then sat in the audience and cried her eyes out. I could not have written this book without all the ways she has helped me hammer out and refine these ideas.

In the same way, I try to be the loudest clapper in Jen's audience. She is a wonderful teacher, and though she doesn't do full-time ministry, she ministers to other women all the time, on top of being a kick-butt wife and mom. I gave Jen a greeting card years ago that said, "Two Superheroes, No Sidekick." She's had it hung in her kitchen ever since, and I love what it says about our friendship. We break the "wind beneath my wings" stereotype that "girlfriend" movies often sell us: that one person gets to shine and one plays a supporting role. Through this friendship I have come to judge the health of other friendships: the measure of our love for each other is how much we want to see the other succeed.

This concept is called mutual mentoring, in which two people see themselves as different but equal. I'm not your project and you're not mine. Rather, "as iron sharpens iron, so one person sharpens another" (Prov. 27:17). Different gifts. Equal strength.

One Sneaky Outcome of Comparison

I'm not your project and you're not mine. Let's take a moment to think about that.

Growing up, I was often exposed to the "project" model of female friendship. I observed that some women shared their issues with others and were given help and advice—sometimes solicited and sometimes not. Those that gave help and advice rarely asked for it in return.

The message I internalized was that in every relationship, one person had problems, and the other had the goods to fix those problems. I entered most of my relationships wondering which one *I* was. "Are you here to fix me or am I here to fix you?" I would wonder.

Many times, I determined *I* was the fixer. And that worked

pretty well for a while, sometimes for years. In those friendships I didn't necessarily believe I was smarter, better, or more spiritual, but perhaps that my life was manageable and theirs wasn't. They had an illness, a more traumatic childhood, a "broken" family, or a less helpful husband. I might even notice that they had a lot more kids than I did and were getting a lot less sleep. Enter Amanda in her super cape to help. I felt blessed and therefore indebted to God to form relationships with those less blessed than I was. (I hope you are already seeing that this is not going to turn out well for anyone.)

My first fixèe was a junior high friend with an absent dad and a serious illness. Then it was the high school friend with a tough family life, who, frankly, wasn't very nice to me. I actually paid for her date's tux for the prom so she wouldn't have to go alone, which she never knew until maybe, like, now. By my thirties I had developed some more mutual relationships, but at the same time I always had a friend who I believed I was called to help. I would never have articulated it that way, but there it is.

This dynamic was rooted in comparison: Whose issues are worse, mine or hers? The sneaky outcome of this comparison and my response to it was creating not trust, safety, authenticity, and encouragement between us, but competition. Eventually, she had to compete with me to prove she was strong too.

As Cloud and Townsend write in *Safe People*, people who insist on being the strong party in the friendship are unsafe, and their friends will suffer "predictable results." Once a woman has been thoroughly cast in the role of the weaker party, she will eventually begin feeling anger and hostility at the "together one." The final result, say the authors is "feeling the need to compete to reverse the role. The weaker person feels stuck in her role and fights to change it. . . . This pattern also keeps the 'strong' one from growing spiritually and emotionally. . . . If we are always being strong and without needs, we are not growing, and we are setting ourselves up for a very dangerous fall."[2]

I can testify to the truth of this in my life: without fail, each one of these women took my help gratefully for a period of time. They called me things like their "work horse" or their "go-to girl" or "the only one I trust." But then there came a time when suddenly they didn't want my help anymore. Or I failed to offer it in quite the right way and they became angry. Or I overstepped my bounds and tried to help with things they really didn't want help with. Every single one of those relationships ended in me being told off, sometimes with expletives. I sat among the wreckage feeling like the wounded party and wondering what went wrong.

I can now recognize that I really hurt others by acting out this dynamic over and over, stealing their dignity by over-helping and judging them to be less than I was. But I also hurt myself. Focusing on the needs of others kept me from seeing that I was wretched, pitiful, poor, blind, and naked, just like everybody else, needing the very help and healing as much as those to whom I was pouring out. So while I was acting selfless, I was building resentments that no one was intuiting my needs as I was intuiting theirs. I am in need of God's grace, not least of all because my comparison of our issues caused the competition and resentment that ended those relationships.

There's a technical term for the dynamic I've just described: it's called codependency. At the root, codependents mix up the difference between being loved and being needed. Until we allow God to heal us, we think people who don't need us don't love us; people who do need us must love us a lot. This is why you hear a lot about codependents marrying and befriending addicts or people with major personality disorders or mental illness; essentially, people who don't or can't give out a lot of love but who are desperately needy (or opportunistic). The flip side of codependency is this: we believe that people who are strong and don't need rescuing must not love us. So, at our sickest, we might not want our friends and loved ones to be superheroes, because we won't feel loved in those relationships. And until we learn to confess our competitive nature and our deep need for love, we won't be able to have true intimacy.

I thank God with all my heart that he has healed me from this unhealthy approach to relationships and continues to fix the broken parts that caused it. And I pray that any of my sisters reading this who recognize this tendency in themselves will ask him for help, too, and maybe even check out a Codependents Anonymous meeting. Because the joy of loving and being loved by equal partners—free from comparison and the weaker/stronger dynamic—is absolutely as good as I always thought it could be.

Give and Take, Like the Avengers

This is the lesson it took me decades to learn: No one wants to be my project. Or yours. No one wants to be rescued all the time, advised all the time, or helped all the time. Actually, I take it back. Some people *do* want to be rescued all the time. We can go ahead and call those people unsafe, and I warn you not to be the warm body they go to when they need someone to help carry what should be their own daily load.

Healthy, safe friends can both give and take from a relationship. Playing the role of taker all the time is a failure to manage your life, lay down selfishness, and love others. But permanently playing the role of giver is an issue of pride: believing that you have the answers for someone else and refusing to admit that someone might have answers for you. You end up holding down those whom you want to build up, and you miss out on the encouragement you need for yourself.

When I was growing up, there was only one superhero and one bad guy per superhero movie. Perhaps that partially explains my nemesis obsession. But these days, the Marvel movies have shown us that the good-versus-evil genre can have an ensemble cast. Have you heard? Iron Man, Thor, the Hulk, Black Panther, Black Widow, Spiderman, Dr. Strange, and Captain America are all working together, bringing their various strengths and tight outfits to the table. Evil doesn't stand a chance with this crack team on the job.

And you, ladies: there's room for all of you to be super. As women with issues, attempting to have long-term, loving relationships with other women with issues, we can stop trying to figure out whose issues are worse. Confess to Jesus when you find yourself envying someone else's superpower. Allow yourself the privilege of being helped as much as helping. Encourage your way into having a fellow superhero, not a sidekick. She will be the one who will help you get stronger day by day and stand by you when you are weak.

I'm Happy for You. Really.

To sum up: if encouragement is nourishing to healthy relationships, then competition is poison. Freely encourage one another, just as you freely and authentically confess your weaknesses and your need for encouragement.

And finally, try this test to see if the potential superhero friend in your life wants you to be one too: Authentically share your joy. Share the pride you have in your kids' character and yes, even their accomplishments; the comfort you find in your marriage; or the wonderful, God-fearing man you just met. Authentically share

God's faithfulness to you in your business, how it is growing, or a risk you took and how it's paid off. And most of all, authentically share how your relationship with Christ is growing, what he's saying to you, what he's helping you overcome. Let your light shine before your friends, that they might see his work and your good deeds, and glorify your Father in heaven.

As my friend Terry sometimes warns, the wise learn not to call certain people with good news because they will just pee in our Cheerios. (I don't know where she comes up with this stuff.) If we share our joy and it's not well received, there is likely a competitive spirit in this friendship that hopefully can be overcome if we confront it honestly and kindly. But let's also remember to be sensitive.

Don't expect your newly divorced friend to rejoice in the health of your marriage or the friend struggling with infertility to be excited about your pregnancy or the friend who has just been laid off to congratulate you on your raise. When you shine these particular little lights of yours in these scenarios, you've just become the unsafe person. And if your friend suddenly sees you as a nemesis, that will be *your* issue. Add it to your issues list, confess it and ask for forgiveness, and then put your cape back on.

Chapter 8

FUNERALS, BIRTHDAYS, AND BABY SHOWERS

Encouragement in Joy and Grief

If you're depressed I will be there for you.

As everyone knows, depressed people are some of the most boring people in the world. I know this because when I was depressed, people fled. Except my best friends.

I will be there for you during your horrible break-up, or getting fired from your job, or if you're just having a bad couple of months or year. I will hate it and find you really tedious, but I promise I won't abandon you.

—MINDY KALING, *IS EVERYONE HANGING OUT WITHOUT ME? (AND OTHER CONCERNS)*

My childhood best friend, Vicki, lost her father suddenly to a heart attack when we were juniors in college. It was right before my finals week, and I came home from the library to find she had called three times. I was shocked and saddened at the news, and immediately bought a train ticket home to be with her for the funeral and the few days leading up to it.

Vicki's relationship with her dad had always been complicated. Her parents divorced when she was in high school and she didn't see him a lot after that. When he was around, though, he was a character—fun and funny. When I was thirteen, he told me that he hadn't minded converting to Judaism for Vicki's mom, except that he really missed marshmallow Peeps at Easter. He always loved food and cooked fattening comfort dishes with a relish. He made sensationally greasy latkes and Shake-and-Bake pork chops for Hanukkah. Vicki, who is a devout Jew and keeps kosher, denies this.

I helped Vicki with some of the funeral planning, which was about celebrating his life, and those involved said, "Oh, Dad would have loved this," or "That is just sooo Dad." That's what you're going for in a memorial, creating an event that your loved one would agree represented their essence. It's hard to do when you feel your deceased deserved sainthood, and even harder when you have mixed feelings about a parent who has passed.

My clearest memory from those days with Vicki was walking through Target, looking for something in which to put her dad's ashes. Urns are very expensive, and the family had decided they were going to find a more utilitarian solution. We eventually bought a stainless-steel cookie jar. That may sound totally irreverent, but Vicki's dad *was* irreverent. When Vicki said at the checkout counter, "Dad would have loved this," she was absolutely right.

I didn't help plan another funeral for two decades, and this time it was my paternal grandmother's. Grandma Bev was an amateur painter. She also loved needlepoint. I was put in charge of decorations for the reception, and I used various items she had made for the family as centerpieces. We looked around and thought with satisfaction that the room reflected her life: the works of her hands and the love for her family.

That same year, Jen's father passed away. Jen did him honor by arranging a potluck of all the family's favorite holiday dishes, and the centerpiece of the buffet was the chassis of a vintage BSA motorcycle. His great love was restoring anything mechanical, especially British-made motorbikes. He would have laughed to see this once-worn-out hunk of metal shined up, with a vase of flowers set on the gas tank.

As I drove home from that memorial, I thought about honoring the people we love. In all these memorials, friends and families—dysfunctional and otherwise—came together to agree on the essential qualities of the one they lost. What was he/she really about and how could they show that they recognized it? I wondered what it would look like if we made an effort to do that for our loved ones before they died. Wouldn't that be an ultimate form of encouragement? I see you, I know you, and I have decorated all these party tables with what you most love.

Sometimes We Give What We Hope to Get

When Gary Chapman wrote *The Five Love Languages*, he didn't include party planning as one of the ways people say, "I love you." But that's mine. I suppose you could say it's a combination of Gifts and Acts of Service, which *are* in Chapman's book.[1] If you are getting married or having a baby or celebrating a decade birthday, I will throw you a killer bash. I will meditate on what you are about: your favorite colors and foods, your hobbies, your mission, and what you love best in life. Then all my errand-running for a month will include finding accessories to support the theme of You. I will make you a cake with which you will want to take pictures: I have made volcanoes and hula dancers, a monster truck track, a sand castle, a clothesline hung with baby onesies, and cupcakes with chocolate butterflies. For Jen's fortieth birthday I did a whole dessert table in black and white to match the brocade tablecloth of her Spain-themed fiesta.

One definition of encouragement is "to give support and advice to (someone) so that they will do or continue to do something." Throwing someone a party that celebrates them is, to me, an ultimate form of encouragement because it supports them in continuing to do the most important thing: being themselves. It says, "On your birthday, friend, I celebrate who God has made you to be and how you continue to do it, better and better every year. Here is a cake in the shape of your favorite hobby. Keep on going, girl."

In *The Five Love Languages*, Chapman tells us something profound: we tend to love other people with the language we wish would be spoken to us. I realized eventually, as a true codependent, that part of me was throwing the party I always wanted for myself. So for my fortieth birthday, I threw *myself* an Amanda party. It was a Western Fortieth Fiesta with line dancing. I made the decorations, the food, the perfect playlist. My brother hosted in his backyard, my mom bought margaritas. My husband special-ordered a piñata shaped like a cowgirl boot. And Jen ordered an enormous tiered cake and put a little wooden version of me, dressed in my western dress and cowgirl boots, on top.

I got the kind of encouragement I needed—country music, photo-ready cake, and cowgirl boots. But the bigger gift I got on my fortieth birthday was a revelation: I had spent many years loving others in my own language. Had I also asked them what language would encourage them most?

I believe the most important part of encouraging someone is to really see them and show that you see them. It's universal: we want to be known and celebrated, for it to matter that we are here on this earth. (My beloved Josie, on my birthday, always gives me a card or a text that says, "I'm glad you were born." It makes me happy.) We go through a lot of crud together in this life. I think we should make an extra effort to celebrate the good stuff. The apostle Paul agrees with me. He says, "Rejoice with those who rejoice" (Rom. 12:15).

Your best friend might not need a themed birthday cake and a color-coded bash. But do you know what she really *would* love? Have you asked her? In my family of origin, holidays and occasions really mattered: graduations, baptisms, showers, and birthdays were important moments to show love. If your friends feel this way, too, you can really hurt them by failing to see these moments as priorities. On the other hand, you could also put a lot of time and money into big celebrations that don't matter so much to your loved ones and miss being there in the small moments that they see as significant.

There's another lesson here too: my friends celebrated my fortieth birthday with me—and Jen got me a stellar cake—because I asked them to. We talked in earlier chapters about the importance of being honest. Can we be honest about what we want? I think we should try. I read in the Old Testament that the sin of the women among the patriarchal families was manipulation (helping sons steal their brother's blessings, sending their husbands to impregnate mistresses, etc.). They tried to bring about what they wanted behind the scenes without being honest and direct. In the New Testament, even Martha, slaving away making roast goat for Jesus, doesn't ask Mary for help but tattles on her to Jesus.

If your birthday is important to you and you want to celebrate it, tell your girlfriends. Ask them honestly and directly to show up for you. As an adult, you have to accept it if they say they can't. James 4:2 says to ask God for what you need, because if you don't ask, you won't receive. If we need to speak our needs to God, who knows everything, how much more do we need to be brave enough to share our hopes and requests with our girlfriends, who can't read our minds?

Encouragement in Grief

You likely know the scripture. Paul didn't just say to rejoice with those who rejoice, but also to mourn with those who mourn. Most of us want to encourage our close friends in times of sorrow, but we tend to think of encouragement as taking on the role of cheerleader: helping someone cheer up, buck up, get moving, keep going. Cheerleaders are good for football games and when friends are suffering from writer's block (thanks to my J's for helping me through this). But they are not appropriate at funerals or in hospital waiting rooms.

One form of encouragement is to literally help a friend bravely face fearful situations. And I'd like to suggest that grieving takes a lot of courage. So sometimes our best encouragement to a friend is to sit with them while they face something overwhelming, horrific, or painful, without trying to take that pain away.

The Jews have a tradition called "sitting *shiva*," a practice observed in different ways by different sects of Judaism, and goes all the way back to the book of Job, the most ancient book of the Bible. *Shiva* means *seven*, and the original practice of sitting *shiva* meant that on the occasion of the death of a parent, child, sibling, or spouse, one would sit in the deceased's home for seven days. Literally, the mourner would sit on a low box or a stool to signify that they had been brought low by sorrow, and in that low state they would receive other mourners, close friends and family who would sit *shiva* with them. Some Jews would wear a torn black ribbon as an outward sign of sorrow, or clothing torn over the heart. In modern times, many Jews still observe this practice, though sometimes only for one to three days, and often in different homes at the same time, since families are spread throughout the world.

Sitting *shiva* gives structure in the first days of grief. Modern psychologists confirm the traditional belief that a mourner should not be distracted from their grief but allowed to be brought low by it for a period of time. Without a formal mourning period, delayed grief can transform into long-term chronic depression.

Our culture is not very good at mourning. It's not even very good at just being plain old sad. In America, "the pursuit of happiness" is in our most prized historical literature. But sometimes, sad is what we really need to be. And if we push sad aside, it may be internalized until we experience low-grade or even acute depression and anxiety for long periods of time.

Again, it takes courage to grieve. In *A Grief Observed*, C. S. Lewis says, "No one ever told me that grief felt so like fear. I am not afraid, but the sensation is like being afraid. The same fluttering in the stomach, the same restlessness, the yawning. . . . There is a sort of invisible blanket between the world and me. I find it hard to take in what anyone says. . . . Yet I want the others to be about me. I dread the moments when the house is empty."[2] Many grieving people or clinically depressed people are afraid. One aspect of the fear is that if they allow themselves to really go down in the depths of their pain, they will never come out of it.

We, their friends and loved ones, may reinforce that fear by trying to advise, soothe, and cheer them up, giving the message that we are afraid they won't come out of it either. Allowing people to be sad, and to even sit on the floor with them while they feel sad, makes us very uncomfortable. We might be overwhelmed, feeling their grief too. Our ultimate fear may be that they will lose their faith, cease to trust in God. And further, I love how honest the author, scriptwriter, and actress Mindy Kaling is in the quote at the top of this chapter: Sad people can be really tedious, so we are also afraid of being stuck in an endless cycle of being sad along with them.

Sitting in Sadness Serves a Spiritual Purpose

The spiritual truth is that Jesus will comfort those who mourn. Take a moment and absorb that in your heart: it's a promise Jesus made to us. The psychological truth is that how our hearts and minds work is counterintuitive: rushing sorrow makes it last longer, and hiding it from others keeps joy at bay.

The Disney Pixar movie *Inside Out* illustrates this brilliantly. *Inside Out*'s main character is eleven-year-old Riley, who has moved away from her friends, her home, and her precious hockey team because of a new job her dad has taken across the country. Her parents tell her they "need" her to be happy. Inside her brain, emotions are personified in the brain's command center. Sadness is kind of an off-putting drag, and Joy tries to make her stand inside a tiny circle so she can't influence Riley's brain. Throughout the movie, we watch what happens as Sadness is banished: Joy gets banished with her. Left in control of Riley's brain are Anger, Fear, and Disgust. It's not until the end of the movie (spoiler alert) that Joy personified realizes, along with Riley's parents, that until Riley is allowed to feel and express her sadness, she can't receive the comfort she needs that will restore her joy.

Two psychologists were consulted by Pixar in the making of the film, Dacher Keltner and Paul Ekman. Ekman traveled the world and discovered six scientifically verified universal emotions (Pixar only had room for five characters in their script, so "Surprise" is left out). Though many of us were taught that our feelings were not to be trusted and expressing them would derail our lives, Ekman's research revealed that our emotions actually help order our rational thinking and also bring order to our social interactions. Say Keltner and Ekman in an article they penned about the movie, "In real life, one person's sadness pulls other people in to comfort and help."[3] Every mom I know who saw that movie cried when Riley's mom and dad finally recognize how sad she is, and they all fall to the kitchen floor in a big family hug: a mixture of empathy and shared sadness, infused with the joy of being together.

Many of us are afraid our sadness will turn people away, so isolating when we are grieving is one of our common issues. But we can help each other heal. To imbue one another with courage (to encourage), we have to be brave enough to let our friends grieve—or even just let them experience run-of-the-mill sadness and frustration, which are part of life. We need courage to sit with them while they are brought low, both metaphorically and sometimes physically, to stop trying to fix and rush them. To just sit until the work of grief is done. And then in turn, we have to be brave enough to share when we need comfort as well.

Here's What Would Help Me

In this season of my life, I have a friend going through a brutal divorce. I want to fix it so badly. When she sends me sad texts on Saturday, missing her kids who are off with their dad, sometimes I want to muscle her out of her loneliness with practical advice. Sometimes I tell her to go out and have fun (this might sometimes *be* good advice). But mostly I remember, prayerfully, that her journey of healing is going to be on her and God's timing, so mostly my job is to listen.

In the middle of this internal struggle one day, I called Josie. We agreed: we couldn't solve the other friend's problem. And then we got to talking about what *we* would want someone to do for *us* in the same situation.

Here's what I told Josie I would want. I would want her to come sit *shiva*. If I face tragedy—such as the loss of my husband or one of my children, God forbid—I don't want to be alone in the first stages of shock, even if I say I do. I might not want to talk, but I want her in the house near me, as C. S. Lewis said. And then in the months afterward when it's time for me to reenter the world, she can help me in the following ways: Come over, make me get dressed, and take me to Home Goods where we can browse and buy something seasonal in my favorite color. Then she can buy me my favorite coffee drink and take me to a movie (cathartic to help us cry maybe, or maybe something to make us laugh). Josie promised she would do it. And she said she'd throw in a pedicure.

Today, I could cry with the relief of having made this plan and having at least one of my J's committed to caring for me in the future, which I will surely need. Eleven years ago, when I was struggling with acute postpartum depression, I was not as adept as I am now at discerning safe relationships. At that time, I was spending my time primarily with one friend. I asked her for help: to get together for one outing a week because I felt so fearful leaving the house with my small daughters alone. She said no.

More precisely, she said that I needed to make some new friends, that I was expecting too much of her. At this point, I had probably really burned her out with all my suffering. She was also a mother of young children with her own issues to deal with; she didn't have the bandwidth to help me at that time. But I took her advice, in a way. I didn't make new friends; I reached out to my old ones. Josie was serving as a missionary in Ukraine, but she supported me in the ways she could: via email, via Skype, and in prayer. Kelly, my other college roommate, had just had a baby and was struggling with

PPD. Somehow we found comfort in knowing that we were in this together, and we prayed together and for each other often. Jen was in the midst of her own personal crisis at the time, so I hadn't turned to her; but then in desperation, I did. And she not only responded with grace and understanding, but with thanksgiving. She was blessed that though I saw the issues she was struggling with, I didn't count her as too broken to help me.

My life has totally changed in the last ten years: I have invested in friends both new and old who are capable of helping me in crises large and small. I now have a network of women who come to my aid in sorrow. And they can count on me too. I've been there for them in hospital waiting rooms and on living room floors. Among these dear ones, we have learned that the secret is to have enough friends that we can spread both our sadness and crazy around. Not one of us expects the other to be their only encourager. Rather, I might do a modern over-the-phone version of sitting *shiva* with Jen in the morning, giving her courage to face her reality. And then head off to dinner with Josie at night so she can encourage me. These are the same women who showed up, in western dress, to my fortieth cowgirl party, ready to boogie even though they don't like country music. Now those are true friends.

This is life in the human heart: joy turning to sadness and then sadness rolling back around to joy. This insight was brought to you by scientific research via Disney Pixar in 2015 and outlined in the Bible two thousand years earlier. We all need those who love us enough to encourage us whether we are celebrating or grieving. And now's the time, ladies: "Don't give up meeting together as some are in the habit of doing, but encourage each other, even more as you see the day approaching" (Heb. 10:25, my paraphrase). Throw each other parties. Go to your friend's loved one's funeral. Give each other courage to keep going.

Part 3

ACCOUNTABILITY

George: You are a good friend. You know what? Even if you
killed somebody, I wouldn't turn you in.

Jerry: Is that so? Hey, Kramer, if I killed somebody, would you
turn me in?

Kramer: Definitely.

—*SEINFELD*, "THE POSTPONEMENT"

And we urge you, brothers and sisters, warn those who
are idle and disruptive, encourage the disheartened,
help the weak, be patient with everyone.

—1 THESSALONIANS 5:14

Chapter 9

TELL ME THE TRUTH

Adventures in Accountability

It takes a great deal of bravery to stand up to our enemies,
but just as much to stand up to our friends.

—J. K. ROWLING, *HARRY POTTER AND THE SORCERER'S STONE*

When my friend Josie and I were in our early twenties, I was already married and Josie was not. As a female who knew she wanted to get married and have children from age, like, six, I had been fortunate. I met my solid, sweet Christian husband when I was only eighteen and married him just before I turned twenty-two. Josie, also a woman who wanted to get married and have children (I note this because not all women *do* want these things), had not yet been so fortunate. And her issue, from my perspective, was that she kept dating guys who weren't marriage material for a Christian girl: they didn't believe in God, and they didn't demonstrate integrity. Though I know there are successful interfaith marriages out there, I cannot imagine enduring the trials of real life and marriage if my husband and I weren't on the same page about our faith. And integrity means we're honest with ourselves and others. I recognize that even men (and women) who claim to follow God don't actually show integrity, which is the most important thing (in my humble opinion) when picking a partner of any kind: spouse, business partner, ministry partner, or friend.

I spent a certain amount of energy for a season encouraging Josie that she was of great worth, so she should hold out for the right kind of guy. I tried to be gracious and loving, if persistent, in this and even sometimes put it to her in song. My fellow sisters of the 1990s might remember Lauryn Hill's hit song "That Thing." One time I actually stuck my head in Josie's car window and sang a line of it to her as she backed out of a mall parking space, a line that reminded her she was a special gemstone and not a regular old rock, so she should find a guy who was worthy of her.

Looking back, I'm grateful that Josie kept hanging out with me, and kept listening to me, though it took her a while to follow my advice. She ended up marrying a missionary and theology professor, then spent more than a decade serving God with him in Kiev, Ukraine, where they had three sons. (Though I have to tell you, I have just discovered that her husband backs into parking spaces. For Josie, thankfully, this is not an issue.)

Adventures in Accountability

Though I can't take even 20 percent of the credit for Josie's happy ending, I consider it an accountability success story, appropriate as we begin examining the third element of building remarkable relationships among imperfect people: adventures in accountability.

We hear the term *accountability* used for public officials, politicians, and corporate leaders. In the news, we often read about a lack of accountability, how someone is trying to weasel their way out of taking blame, and we, the public, insist that high-level officials should have to answer to someone. But in friendships, accountability simply means inviting those we know and love best to tell us when we are acting unwisely and against our standards of character. I knew Josie's goal was to marry a man of faith; therefore, I could comfortably speak up when she was taking steps in the opposite direction.

I like applying the word *adventure* to something that sounds as serious as accountability because it adds a measure of fun. *Adventure* also implies inherent danger. In *Indiana Jones* movies, the hero and his love interest will endure some experiences that will make us, the audience, wonder how they will possibly make it out alive. At the end of the film, Indie will look a little worse for wear, though, inexplicably, the female lead will still be wearing lip gloss.

Embarking on accountability adventures with our friends, issues and all, *is* a brave undertaking, one in which there may be conflict and the danger even of an end to the relationship. Proverbs 9:7–8 says, "Do not reprove a scoffer, lest he hate you. Reprove a wise man, and he will love you." Sometimes you can't tell who's a wise woman and who is a scoffer until you've tried pointing out where she might be going slightly askew. It's like a *Temple of Doom* booby trap. But also, as for Indiana Jones, there is treasure to be found in this adventure. The practice of holding each other accountable yields the amazing joy of becoming kinder, wiser, less obnoxious people.

In chapter 2 I shared that my friend Jen regularly prays this courageous prayer, "Show me the truth about myself," and the result of this spiritual practice is that she's a woman aware of her issues and capable of healthy change. Also, during one of our frequent phone calls, in which we share our challenges with coworkers, husbands, children, neighbors, baristas, pastors, and kids' soccer coaches, we will say to the other this brave sentence: "Okay, tell me the truth." Or, at other times, we ask, "Is this *my* issue?"

I'm so grateful to have a trusted friend whom I can ask this question. Jen knows that I struggle with impatience and worry, that I can be passive aggressive, and that when I'm feeling really hurt, I come off as angry (and like the Incredible Hulk used to say, "You wouldn't like me when I'm angry"). Since I don't have to hide my flaws with her, Jen is in a unique place to point them out and help me work on them. This system is one of the best tools I have to become the person God wants me to be.

Are You Asking for Feedback?

I want to be kind, loving, patient, and gentle. But inside, sometimes I'm still a selfish, wounded seven-year-old who is upset that things aren't all about me. I recently heard a woman with a PhD in psychology explain how when we get triggered by upsetting circumstances, the functioning of our prefrontal cortex ceases, and we begin operating in our brain stem, the source of emotion; this is how children react to stress because their prefrontal cortexes aren't yet developed.

When I've gone into my brain stem, I call Jen, Gina, or Josie (sometimes all three). They are safe enough to see me in seven-year-old mode, when I'm in a rage, in despair, petty, frustrated, consumed by a wound or offense, or overwhelmed with a disappointment. They aren't perfect, but they receive my mess with grace, and gosh I love them for it. Because these are the moments when I'm most likely to act against my own standards of integrity and get myself into trouble.

I receive their messes in turn. In these exchanges, we use this essential friendship tool: we ask the question, "Are you asking for feedback?" It makes the adventure of accountability less dangerous for everyone. We know we can answer, "No, I don't want feedback; I just want to vent," and that is totally allowed. At times, I have said no to hearing friends' constructive advice and insights and, instead, finished my vent. They validate Child Amanda's feelings and confirm that I am not a terrible, wicked person, but a hurt person. Then I get to cry. Then I get to feel better.

The friends then store that raw information for later, when I'm saner, to help me understand myself and grow as a human being. They can remind me to ask myself, *What harmful attitudes am I holding that might contribute to all this rage? What do I need to repent of? How can I have better boundaries so I don't get myself in this situation again?*

I feel like maybe I've lost some of you. You're thinking this is not an adventure you want to go on. You may even be thinking, *No way. I'm not that emotional. And even if I was, no one needs to see it.*

But I'm going to push you hard on this one, sisters. Because I don't want you to be alone when you're overwhelmed, which sometimes happens to all of us. I don't want you to make rash decisions that have lasting effects on your life because no one was around to tell you to stop. You need someone who knows you at your most emotional and doesn't run the other way. Because these raw moments reveal important things about our character that are in need of attention.

Single women, you need this, because you don't have someone to see you lose your crap in the kitchen when you have a bad phone conversation with your sister/brother/boss/other friend. You have to radically invite someone to know you like this.

Married women, you need this, because though you do have a man in the house to see you get ugly, some of that ugly is toward him. I don't care how great your marriage is or how holy you are, you're going to need someone other than him to tell you when your heart is not right about your husband, when the issue is yours, not his. You also need the perspective of a friend who can hear about your problems with your in-laws and loves you, but is not so vested in the solution that they can't just hang up and go on with their day when they're through talking to you. Jen's husband and mine are very, very grateful that we have each other for these reasons.

Mothers, you need this because you love your kids more than your own life, but sometimes you want to kill them. You need to be able to say that to someone who understands and doesn't judge you. But who then can tell you the truth about where you might be getting things wrong.

Single mothers, you really, really need this, because you have the hardest job in the world. If I were parenting alone, I'd probably be an alcoholic, and I'm not making a joke. You need to be able to call another adult when you are crazy frustrated and in despair so they can both encourage you and kick your butt, so you can do a good job as a mama. What other choice do you have?

To Whom Are We Accountable, and Who Needs to Remind Us?

If you've been around church for a significant amount of time, you've also heard the concept of "holding each other accountable." You may have even had an accountability partner, someone whose job it was to check up on you and make sure you followed through on a spiritual goal or discipline, or in abstaining from a particular sin. There's a general understanding in modern churches that we are supposed to help one another be "holy," yet accountability is one of the most confusing concepts for Christians.

Foundationally, accountability in our spiritual lives comes from knowing *to whom* we are answering. If you claim to be a follower of Jesus, the answer is to Jesus, not to our friends' opinions or preferences. Though many concepts in this book apply to friends who aren't Christians, the ones in this section won't, and we need to remember what Paul says in 1 Corinthians 5:12: "What business is it of mine to judge those outside the church?"

In the context of Christian friendships, rebuking sin is one of the most loving things you can do, because God's law is good, "making wise the simple," and following it keeps us out of a lot of trouble (Ps. 19:7). Helping our sisters walk in God's ways is to show a holy affection for their well-being. First Peter 2:9 says, "You are a chosen people, a royal priesthood, a holy nation, God's special possession, that you may declare the praises of him who called you out of darkness into his wonderful light." We want to encourage our friends to be the full expression of their identity in Christ, and they can't do this while walking in the habitual darkness of sin. I've experienced personally the benefits of Proverbs 28:23—"In the end, people appreciate honest criticism far more than flattery"—having been both the criticized and the honest (but loving, I hope) critic.

We have to know God's law to correct people on matters of God's law. If you feel uneasy about something a dear friend is up to and think maybe you should speak up, check that feeling against Scripture to see if the unease is due to an overactive conscience and otherwise skewed perception, or on God's concrete truth. If you and I are friends, there are a few things I will call you out on and feel scripturally justified in doing:

- If you're lying routinely to your husband, your boss, your family, or me. (Because God is truthful, and Satan is the father of lies.)

- If you're cheating on your husband or getting dangerously close to it through a flirtation at work, at church, or in your neighborhood. (Because adultery is bad, man, and hurts everyone involved.)
- If you are looking at or reading pornography, alone or with your spouse. (Jesus warns about lust, even in the heart, and pornography is addictive.)
- If you're engaging in gossip, especially about other women in the church. And you're going to have to call me out, too, because this is a major temptation. (Proverbs 16:28 says, "A perverse person stirs up conflict, and a gossip separates close friends.")

There are a few on this list that I've been called out on too. And I'm guessing that even if you don't believe the Bible is a source of truth or aren't really sure how you feel about Jesus (I'm glad you're here, by the way, and thanks for sticking with me so long), you see the wisdom of keeping your friends from a few items on this list, too, which are essentially issues of integrity.

Rebuke Is Loving, Restoration More So

Though the conflict-averse among us may shy away from pointing out a friend's unwise behavior, some of us Christians can get a little overzealous about it. The New Testament uses words like *rebuke*, *teach*, and *warn* about a dozen times, and I've seen women in the church really latch onto those verses. But context is important. These instructions were usually written to teachers like Timothy, Titus, and the elders of a church and were to be used in writing and teaching their congregation as a whole. They were also given to those who have been acknowledged by their faith community as being wise and possessing spiritual gifts of teaching or shepherding.

Therefore, these scriptures don't give license for each of us to go running around rebuking people willy-nilly, nor do they point to a responsibility for each individual Christian to call out the sin of every woman she meets in a small-group Bible study. That's what close friendships are for.

My pastor Kenton Beshore once said, "If you're not going to be part of the restoration, don't be part of the rebuke." I love his perspective, drawn from Galatians 6:1: "Brothers and sisters, if someone is caught in a sin, you who live by the Spirit should restore that person gently. But watch yourselves or you also may be tempted."

"Restore gently" is the most significant phrase in this passage, because harsh rebukes are both unmerciful and typically ineffective, making us too defensive to receive them. Our issues, bad habits, and sinful patterns are almost never about only wickedness or willfulness, but wounds and unmet emotional needs. So when a friend is "caught in sin" and you know their issues, history, and current struggles, be ready to restore through listening, encouragement, and prayer for their release from the trap, as well as holding a hard line of holiness.

Second most important is "watch yourself." As a young Christian, I thought this meant I might be tempted to the very sin I was addressing in someone else. I was wrong. I am much more likely to succumb to the temptation of pride and judgmentalism. As I shared in chapter 7, my issues run to codependency, in which I cast myself in the role of fixer in friends' lives. When I bring up an issue I see as a problem, I have to be very careful to stay humble and not try to control how they do or do not take my advice. Jesus also said that we are prone to picking out the speck of sawdust in a friend's eye while ignoring the plank in our own (Matt. 7:5). Continuing to bring my own issues to Jesus helps me remember that he is the Savior and I am still the imperfect human in this scenario.

My friendships are the means by which God is working out this issue of judgmentalism in my life as he calls us to *mutual* accountability. If Gina just pointed out a way I was unkind to my husband last week, I'm less likely to get puffed up and cheeky when I point out something unhealthy she's up to this week. Mutual accountability keeps us from thinking of ourselves as "She Who Is Spiritual" while casting a friend in the role of "She Who Is Worthy of Rebuke." I recommend that you actually talk about this. "Let's make a deal," you might say to a friend. "I'll tell you when I see you getting loose in the turns, and you do the same for me."

Which leads us to this conclusion: accountability within the healthiest friendships is organic and relational, accomplished by doing life together authentically. When we surround ourselves with women we believe are wise, whose values and opinions we respect, and whose love for us is secure, we usually end up living to a higher calling even if they never outwardly rebuke us.

The good news is that as we practice these principles, the calling out gets less frequent and about fewer major issues. There was a season that I tried to influence Josie for good in her choice of life partner. That season has been over for fifteen years, and I don't think I've felt convicted to point out any unwise behavior to her since.

Boundaries and Accountability

When "someone is caught in a sin," one of the best ways to love them is to refuse to do it with them. Don't drink with a friend who is drinking too much or gossip with a friend who gossips. Don't shop with a friend who is burying herself in debt and/or lying to her husband about it. Rebuke a married friend who is engaging in an office flirtation, and then refuse to hear about it from then on. This may be the part of the adventure where the audience gasps and wonders if your relationship is going to make it. At this point, trust your most important relationship: the one with Jesus, who loves you *and* your friend more than anyone else does.

My favorite movie of all time is *When Harry Met Sally*. Sally's best friend is Marie (Carrie Fisher), who is carrying on an affair with a married man. Screenwriter Nora Ephron (my hero) never shows us Marie and the guy together; she only shows us Marie's conversations about it with Sally. Here's one:

> **Marie:** So I just happened to see his American Express bill.
> **Sally:** What do you mean you just "happened" to see it?
> **Marie:** Well, he was shaving and . . . there it was in his briefcase?
> **Sally:** What if he came out and saw you looking through his briefcase?
> **Marie:** You're missing the point, I'm telling you what I found. He just spent a hundred and twenty dollars on a new nightgown for his wife. I don't think he's ever going to leave her.
> **Sally:** No one thinks he's ever going to leave her.
> **Marie:** You're right, you're right. I know you're right.[1]

Sally delivers her line, "No one thinks he's ever going to leave her," in a way that any woman can tell, she has said this same thing to her friend over and over again. Sally is done convincing Marie that she's in a bad situation. Now she's just on "broken record" mode, and she's not going to further engage in a crazy-making conversation.

I think Sally's approach makes sense: there's a point where you have said what you think is true, and now you hold the line without emotion.

We've probably all been in a position like Sally's. What do we do when we call someone out with the best intentions—prayerfully, gently, and with the hope to restore—and they won't receive correction or alter their path but forge foolishly ahead?

Healthy accountability then has to incorporate good boundaries. After the command to restore the one caught in sin, in Galatians 6, Paul writes, "Carry each other's burdens, and in this way, you will fulfill the law of Christ. If anyone thinks they are something when they are not, they deceive themselves. Each one should test their own actions. Then they can take pride in themselves alone, without comparing themselves to someone else, for each one should carry their own load" (vv. 2–5).

Holding up the standard of moral accountability in the body of Christ appears, in this context, to be a shared burden in our community. At the same time, Paul calls each of us to carry our own load: our daily toil, our personal responsibilities. In *Boundaries*, Cloud and Townsend also define our own load as our choices, emotions, and desires (among other things). So, while trying to point out a loved one's sin is our burden to bear and our spiritual responsibility, forcing them to actually make that choice is *not*.

We can't control others, but we can control ourselves. Here are three possible choices we can make when our friends are engaging in a destructive and/or clearly sinful pattern.

- Refuse to be with them when they are engaging in a destructive behavior ("I won't double date with this guy who is verbally abusing you"; "I can't have a glass of wine with you now that I've expressed my concerns that you are drinking too much.")

- Refuse to receive confidences about the destructive behavior ("You know how I feel about this situation. I don't want to talk about it anymore.")

- Take a break from the friendship while this behavior is going on ("It's hurting me too much to spend time with you while you are on this path.")

If I were Sally, I'd be taking the third option with Marie. I believe the marriage vow is sacred, and I won't walk closely with someone who is actively conducting an affair. Sally, however, does what many well-meaning friends would do: she tries to fix the situation by setting Marie up with Harry; in the movie, this ultimately works out. (Kind of. Marie falls in love with Harry's best friend.) But in real life this is crossing a boundary and trying to take control of her friend's love life. We'd have to call that conduct codependent, and it would likely be unsuccessful.

These kinds of issues are turning points in friendships. When we choose not to listen to or participate in unhealthy behaviors, the friendship might end, or pause for a season. This is a heartbreaking path I've walked. I've also walked a path on which I stayed close to a friend I knew was getting herself into trouble because I thought I was the only one keeping her from going off the cliff. It didn't go well for anyone. My friends, Jesus is the one who saves, not us. So, rebuke, comfort, and attempt to restore. And then don't force the issue. Don't stay around to babysit, nag, and otherwise control another adult friend's behavior. Even God doesn't do this. Instead he gives people the dignity of making their own choices. Say your piece and then keep your peace, trusting that God will continue to speak in your silence.

Nobody's Perfect (Have We Established That Yet?)

I had a woman in my life growing up that I watched constantly dumping friends. When they'd try to give her perspective or advice, she would say things like, "How can she tell me what to do? Doesn't she realize she has issues in her marriage/with her kids/at work/with housekeeping/etc.?"

She was demanding not just perfection from her friends but perfect self-awareness, and she was assuming that they couldn't recognize anything accurately in her because they didn't know everything about themselves. To this woman, myself, and you, I say this: self-awareness is necessary in a friend, but total self-awareness is not possible for anyone. Demanding it from friends will ensure that we live our lives alone. And demanding perfection from those who hold us accountable is a cop-out; they don't always have to be right to tell us when we are wrong.

I have spent a lot of time in my life walking around with blind sides. My friends have seen things in me I couldn't see in myself. It's like this: I can see myself in the mirror, but they can see me from the back. We all have had tags sticking out of the backs of our shirts, or our skirts caught in our pantyhose. That's why we keep each other around, not because we have it all together, but because we need people who tell us when our bums are hanging out.

Chapter 10

THE YEAR EVERYONE GOT A BOOB JOB

Accountability in the Face of Individuality

> Dione and I are friends because we both know what it's like
> to have people be jealous of us.
>
> —CHER IN *CLUELESS*

There are many ways in which my hometown in Orange County, California, is not like *The Real Housewives of Orange County*. We are not all rich or dramatic, nor do we all wear so much eyeliner. However, women in the OC, especially in certain coastal cities, do tend to try to fit a certain image. When they wear yoga pants, it's because they actually went to yoga. Just after they went to CrossFit. They get back into their skinny jeans pretty fast after having babies, and their hair is usually sleek and professionally processed.

Plastic surgery is not Brazil-popular, but it is big. As are women's cup sizes, which are easy to see since they are all wearing yoga tops. Even in my church's MOPS group, over the breakfast buffet, a friend and I used to giggle, "Put the girls away, mamas! It's only nine in the morning."

I was never what you'd call voluptuous, even before I got pregnant. After I finished breastfeeding my last child, I was even less so. My old clothes hung loosely; I felt like a washed-up old lady, or perhaps a teenage boy. It was like a death had occurred, and I was in deep mourning. I began to ask my husband if perhaps we had seven to ten thousand dollars laying around so I could have elective surgery.

"Wouldn't you rather go to Europe?" he said. (I should perhaps mention here that my husband is a leg man.)

Since we didn't have the money for Europe *or* surgery, I tried to resign myself to the situation. I was literally so sad about this perceived loss of beauty that I took it to Jesus in prayer. I asked for contentment. Within a week, God led me to this scripture, Proverbs 5:18–19:

> May your fountain be blessed,
> and may you rejoice in the wife of your youth.
> A loving doe, a graceful deer—
> may her breasts satisfy you always,
> may you ever be intoxicated with her love.

This passage is offering counsel to men as they age to stay with the wives they married, and not go find other young woman when their first wife gets older (sadly, the lack of heeding this counsel is another way in which my hometown *is* like *Real Housewives*). I marveled at the way God's Word can be applied to odd and edgy subjects. I thought, *Well, God knows what happens to breasts when we get older, and he's telling my husband to be content, as well as me.* I felt both convicted and comforted.

And then something awful happened. A very close friend (note: I'm not using her name because this is one of those intimate moments we discussed in chapter 1), also suffering post-nursing, got a boob job. Then a childhood friend, a girl with whom I had attended Sunday school, got one too. Finally, my closest friend in MOPS got her breasts done. And now there they were, staring me down in the breakfast buffet. I felt like Kelly Ripa and I were the last flat-chested women left in America. And I also found that I hadn't necessarily outgrown the feelings of adolescence, when it's hard to be the only one standing in your conviction.

It's so hard, in fact, that I started to entertain superior and judgmental thoughts by way of consolation. While my *friends* had spent money and time on vanity, *I* had made a more spiritual decision to be content and listen to God. If any other friends considered this surgery, I would certainly talk them out of it, using my Bible verse as proof!

Oh, dangerous waters, my sisters. Personal conviction should never give way to others' condemnation. But it's difficult. When people close to us make different choices than we do, it can make us doubt our own convictions, which can sometimes get transformed in our mixed-up hearts to a need to convict *them*.

What's Right for One Child of God Might Not Be Right for All of Them

Jesus was a man of mystifyingly diverse instructions. To a rich young ruler, he suggested selling all his possessions and giving to the poor; but to the woman who "wasted" a month's wages on expensive perfume to anoint Jesus' feet, he affirmed the extravagance, saying, "The poor will always be with you, but you will not always have me." Jesus told one potential disciple to follow him immediately, even though it meant skipping his father's funeral; yet he forbade the man delivered from a legion of demons from following, and instead sent him back home to testify to his family.

In all these cases, Jesus had a very good reason for his specific message to each child of God. I believe he continues to speak to his children in this way, like his moral will is the melody and each of us have a different harmony he calls us to sing.

Jen and I have weathered decades of watching God call us to different things at different times. When I was at the height of my modest journalism career, God told me in no uncertain terms to give it up and stay home with my children. Jen, a successful working mother, watched me make that decision with a lot of personal angst. What if God was also asking her to do the same? And wouldn't it be nice to have park playdates if we were both stay-at-home moms? But she felt God's leading and stayed at her job, and today she continues to kick butt at the same company, where she is paid well and has a lot of flexibility because of her long loyalty. In the last decade, I began my speaking business and wrote two books, something I never could have done as a secular journalist; and though our bank account has suffered, my soul is healthier than ever, and I believe I've been in God's will for me. Jen, meanwhile, continues to shine a light for Jesus in her workplace, as well as pursuing ministry in her spare time. *And* her kids have a college fund.

Not only do all my friends have issues, they have individuality. Many of us are on opposite sides of issues that divide nations, churches, and people on Facebook. We are working mothers, stay-at-home mothers, single mothers, married mothers, and women who *aren't* mothers by choice; homeschoolers, public and private schoolers; teachers, missionaries, and marketing strategists; Republicans, Democrats, Independents, and undecideds; iPhone and Android users; Western medicine devotees and alternative medicine advocates; gun owners and anti-gun protest marchers; Presbyterians,

Lutherans, Baptists, and undeclared; vegans, Paleos, carnivores, and cupcake-eaters. With some, I have many convictions in common, and that's as comforting as a Tempur-Pedic mattress. With others, we might debate differences of opinion, but we don't try to force one another to our side. With still others, we now accept our differences with a laugh and an agreement to disagree in few words.

If I or my friends had insisted on homogenizing our convictions, opinions, or callings, our relationships would have lasted months rather than years. I'm so grateful that we've gotten to the place of accepting our diversity. Because in some kind of counterintuitive miracle, their strength and courage of conviction help me stand in mine.

Meanwhile, God continues to offer the encouragement we each need to keep going, even in the odd and edgy things. Last year, at a women's Bible study gathering, a total stranger approached me. I was wearing a yoga top (I had actually been to yoga).

"I hope this doesn't sound weird," she said, "but I just want to affirm you. I love that look: fit arms and small chest."

"No, it doesn't sound weird," I said, though it kind of did, I guess. "It sounds like God's specific encouragement to me."

Babywise and Not So Wise— Checking Our Motivation

In the interest of full disclosure, I have not always been so good at respecting the dignity of others' choices in the face of my own personal convictions. My struggle with my surgically augmented friends was internal. I never voiced concerns. If only that had always been the case. In my twenties I was the queen of the "right answer." I was certain of the correct way to do lots of things, both spiritual and otherwise, and convinced I had the right scriptural interpretation to back it up. I thank God to this day that my first editor didn't fire me, the women in my Bible study tolerated me, and my brother's wife whom he married around that time now actually claims me as family. I just made a formal amends to her a few months ago and she forgave me; I had been a little scary at the Thanksgiving table, apparently.

Becoming a mother helped me understand this issue of personal conviction and how it fits in to the biblical concepts of accountability—and how I was getting it wrong.

It all starts with a book called *Babywise*. *Babywise* was a best-selling book on sleep training: a methodology to get your baby on a regular sleep schedule by the time they are six to eight weeks old. I don't remember who gave me this book, but I read it while pregnant with my first daughter, and it was the first book about baby sleep that I read. It painted a dramatic picture in the first chapter: the *Babywise* infant took regular naps and slept through the night. The *Babywise* mom took showers, put on makeup, did a little sewing, talked on the phone, cooked food for herself and others, and in the interval played with and fed her happy baby. The non-*Babywise* mom was harried, distressed, sleep deprived, isolated, without identity, and one step away from the asylum. Which one would *you* choose?

I set out to *Babywise* that baby if it killed me. And it almost did. It involved a lot of letting my little one "cry it out," which involved a lot of my husband holding me down and reciting a *Babywise* manifesto while I alternately tried to ignore my guilt and wrestle my way out of our room and into the nursery to pick her up. The methodology did work, by gum, and my baby girl slept regularly from early on, allowing me to work from home as a journalist with some modicum of sanity and hygiene intact. She's still an awesome sleeper, in fact, if somewhat overattached to routines.

But I struggled with hanging out with other moms. I joined MOPS at this stage of my life, and there found that many women around the small group tables, and many speakers from the stage, were not *Babywise*-ing their babies. They were doing things like Attachment Parenting, Kangaroo Care, and Child-Directed Breastfeeding, all things *Babywise* condemned as risky if not actually immoral. I found myself either trying to convince other women to use my method (especially if they looked really tired) or choosing to be around only other women who shared my point of view.

Over time I learned an amazing three-part lesson.

1. Almost all the moms I talked to had the same goals: they wanted children who were healthy, well-fed, emotionally stable, securely attached to their parents, and who would grow into independent adults. They just had totally different convictions about how to accomplish those goals. Maybe they just read a different book first?

2. The Bible says very little about sleep training or even child-rearing in general. I began to think about how many subjects on which Christians have strong convictions are not laid out clearly in Scripture. What kind of food we should eat (Keep kosher? Go vegetarian? Eat fish and lamb and grain like Jesus did? Eat all vegetables like Daniel did?). How much screen time should we let our kids have? Should we buy a house or rent an apartment? Should we get married right out of college or wait until we are thirty? Should we vote Republican or Democrat? I'm just scratching the surface here.

3. Possibly most importantly, I learned about my motives. Though I acted as though, and maybe even believed, that I was trying to help others by converting them to my parenting doctrine (can I just make a public apology to all three of

ALL MY FRIENDS HAVE ISSUES

my sisters-in-law right now?), my motive was also fear that I might be doing it wrong. At the core of this behavior was the erroneous belief that only one of us could be right. And so, my campaign to "help" other mothers with sleep training falls under the "what accountability is not" category: it is not to soothe our own anxiety.

So here comes the broad lesson for us in accountability: if we're trying to hold our friends accountable to a standard we've set for ourselves, and our motivation is that it will make *us* feel better about our choice, we need to check that motive and shut our mouths. Such behaviors are usually rooted in (1) selfishness—commonality makes for simpler communion, or (2) insecurity—the fear that only one of you can be right.

Because of point two, even if our motives are truly good, we should heed the wise words of James: "Everyone should be quick to listen, slow to speak and slow to become angry, for human anger does not produce the righteousness that God desires" (1:19–20). Even our so-called righteous anger when we think a friend could be getting it wrong. The most well-known passage on this issue in the New Testament is Romans 14:3–10:

> The one who eats everything must not treat with contempt the one who does not, and the one who does not eat everything must not judge the one who does, for God has accepted them. Who are you to judge someone else's servant? To their own master, servants stand or fall. And they will stand, for the Lord is able to make them stand.
>
> One person considers one day more sacred than another; another considers every day alike. Each of them should be fully convinced in their own mind. Whoever regards one day as special

does so to the Lord. Whoever eats meat does so to the Lord, for they give thanks to God; and whoever abstains does so to the Lord and gives thanks to God. For none of us lives for ourselves alone, and none of us dies for ourselves alone. If we live, we live for the Lord; and if we die, we die for the Lord. So, whether we live or die, we belong to the Lord. For this very reason, Christ died and returned to life so that he might be the Lord of both the dead and the living.

You, then, why do you judge your brother or sister? Or why do you treat them with contempt? For we will all stand before God's judgment seat.

According to Paul, it's unspiritual to try to convert your dear ones to your Paleo diet or your new cash-only way of handling money. And according to me, it's annoying as heck. Live, eat, spend, exercise, educate your kids, and manage your time your way to the glory of Jesus, and let the ones you love do so as well.

But for you control freaks out there (and I recognize you, being one of you), I'd like to let you in on a little secret. When we simply live out our convictions and don't talk about them much, sometimes another counterintuitive miracle occurs. Sometimes our friends come around to our way of thinking after all. They catch on to what we're doing if they see that it works. I like to call this organic accountability. Codependents Anonymous, of which I am a proud attendee, calls this having "a ministry of attraction, not promotion." Jesus called it letting your light shine on a hill. People are much more likely to be influenced by a good example than a lady on a soapbox. So shine your little light and shut your little mouth. Your friends might become a little more like you. Or, irony of ironies, you may find yourself becoming a little more like them.

Chapter 11

GET OFF THE TREADMILL AND
EAT A CUPCAKE ALREADY

Accountability to Wholeheartedness

Look, you're my best friend, so don't take this the wrong
way. In twenty years, if you're still livin' here, comin' over
to my house to watch the Patriots games, still workin' con-
struction, I'll . . . kill you. That's not a threat, that's a fact.
I'll . . . kill you.

—CHUCKIE IN *GOOD WILL HUNTING*

I find the Michelob Ultra beer commercials to be a great source
of inspiration. This low-carb beer is marketed to young people of
exceptional determination and athletic prowess. The commercials
always picture gorgeous men and women getting up early and hit-
ting the gym, running up flights of stairs, riding bicycles, hiking
steep mountains, and leaning into end-of-race ribbons. Then they
show the actors showered and dressed beautifully as they meet up in

the evening to drink a nice, healthy beer together. I get a sense from these mini movies that the nature of this relationship is such that if one of them didn't show up for the fifteen-mile hike or missed their group workout, someone would go shake the delinquent out of bed. But they don't have to do it very often, because just being in each other's community holds them to a high standard. (If you need a good laugh, go Google the Super Bowl Michelob Ultra commercial from 2018 starring Chris Pratt, who is so excited they finally think he's fit enough to be in the commercial, but who ends up only getting to be an extra. Also, if you don't find Chris Pratt pretty darn dreamy, despite what I said in the last chapter about allowing our friends to have different tastes, I don't know if this thing between you and me is going to work out.)

Seriously, though, I think these commercials are effective because they paint a picture of something we deeply desire: a community that has the same goals and helps each other achieve them, because even the most self-motivated among us struggles with lack of self-control and discouragement. When our goals are spiritual in nature—like growing our faith, having healthy relationships or creating anything that shows God's love—we face the added challenge of spiritual warfare. Spiritual warfare often occurs on a mental and emotional level. In other words, the spiritual enemy Jesus taught us about uses our issues to slow us down or cripple us in achieving our goals.

Enter my J's: in my life they are the Jesus-y version of the Michelob Ultra commercial crowd, and together we get drunk on the heady pleasure of seeing the Holy Spirit move powerfully in each other's lives, breaking strongholds, healing our hearts, and allowing us to accomplish both short- and long-term goals. I call this accountability to wholeheartedness. This aspect of accountability is connected to our identity in Christ: urging, encouraging, and in some cases badgering each other to meet our goals, use our gifts, and pursue our God-given callings.

Meeting Goals

Josie was looking to buy her first home after being an overseas missionary for thirteen years. She wanted her first home to be her last home so her family could have stability after years of being expats. I helped her stay accountable to that goal by giving her feedback about the home listings she sent me, which at first were not quite "marriage material." I've been a homeowner for fifteen years, so I could help point out impractical elements of some of the vintage properties she was looking at. Ultimately, she got a great, solid house. In her words, the first few she looked at were like guys she dated in college: flashy and interesting, but not good for the long haul. The house she bought is more like her husband: practical and with a firm foundation. My input (both in husbands and houses, see chapter 9) helped a little in this decision-making process.

In another example, my friend Sophie is an uber-talented entrepreneur who is working on overcoming workaholism and bringing balance to the beautiful life she shares with her husband. When she's taking a long weekend off, she texts me and tells me to hold her accountable to being present with her man. I might check in with her once over the weekend ("Hey, turn off your laptop, girl!"), but more often, she'll text me and say, "I'm feeling anxious about not checking email," and just the act of reaching out to me helps her stay present and stick with it.

Jen is a working mother who likes her job, loves her family, and who also has the gift of teaching and a huge heart to see women find emotional healing through Jesus. When she has to make a decision about signing a new contract with her office or committing to a new ministry endeavor, she calls me to discuss it. I pray for her a lot. I listen. And I help reflect back to her what I think she most desires and try to confirm what she hears God saying to her. I've never said anything like "Quit work!" or "Sign that contract!" but rather keep her accountable to a prayerful decision-making process.

As for me, I've asked several of my friends for help reaching goals in their areas of expertise. Sophie helps me set writing, marketing, and social media goals, then offers me tons of encouragement when I meet them. Gina points out when I'm too focused on the wrong relationships: those that will tax me spiritually and distract me from being present with my precious daughters, or from hearing God while I write. And Josie, with a mind like a steel trap, remembers the revelations God has given me to change my heart and behavior, and reminds me of them as well. (She also corrects my punctuation and spelling and occasionally fact-checks my blog without being asked.)

All these examples are to illustrate an important part of whole-hearted accountability: We set the goals, and our friends offer accountability to these goals. We don't set goals for each other (see the previous chapter), but we depend on one another as a helpful tool for achieving our goals. If you are setting a meaningful goal in your life, don't miss the opportunity to involve your girlfriends in it. Maybe my friends are just bossy, but I find they are almost always willing to push me harder if I ask to be pushed.

Getting Us Off Our Goals

And then there's another kind of accountability I need: to be told when I'm pushing too hard and being a perfectionist.

Author and sociological researcher Brené Brown writes at

length about shame and value, and I share her affection for the concept of living wholeheartedly. In her book *Daring Greatly*, she says it this way:

> Wholehearted living is about engaging in our lives from a place of worthiness. It means cultivating the courage, compassion, and connection to wake up in the morning and think, *No matter what gets done and how much is left undone, I am enough.* It's going to bed at night thinking, *Yes, I am imperfect and vulnerable and sometimes afraid but that doesn't change the truth that I am worthy of love and belonging.*[1]

Amen. I believe I am worthy of love despite my imperfections because of the love of God and the covering of my sins on the cross by the blood of Jesus. I want to pursue goals that are within God's will for me and aligned with his dreams for me, but somehow cling to the truth that my worth is not attached to achievement. But I often fail at this. Even more so, I sometimes set ridiculous goals for myself without consulting with God, and they get me into trouble.

For an example, as I write this chapter, I am on day eleven of a sugar cleanse. I'm cranky. And I'm starving.

Dietary cleanses aren't really my thing, and this sugar detox has been brutal. For the first week I couldn't have carbohydrates at all. When I decided to try this, I enlisted two accountability partners that I could text when I wanted to give up and eat a donut: Sophie and Gina—both of whom eat very clean and healthy and also love me. This second part is key.

Because of this stupid diet, my husband and I had the worst date night ever, in which he ate a succulent platter of fried chicken and duck-fat fries, and I had a "Malibu Barbie on a Bed." (I could not make this up: it was a chicken thigh on a bed of lettuce.) The word *hangry* was coined for me. I was mean and he was irritated. All in all, the evening out was not the relaxing source of connection we both needed.

While on the date, when I texted my accountability partners from the bathroom (of course), they totally surprised me. They didn't say, "Push through, you can do this." Sophie said, "Ease up and have some carbohydrates. Give yourself grace." Gina said, "Have some fries."

And then the next morning, Jen, who knows various other challenging things I'm up to in my life right now, told me it might be wise to wimp out on this diet. (Did you hear the shame in that? That's *not* actually what she said, but it's what I heard.) She asked if maybe I was asking too much of myself, and should I maybe go for moderation in this food thing? She believes in me, she said, that I have the self-control to eat good enough. I don't have to eat "perfect."

Because Gina, Sophie, and Jen know me so well, they can offer me the accountability I need, sometimes even more than the accountability I ask for. They know that I am prone to perfectionism, legalism, and pride. Jen specifically refocused me on the important things God is calling me to and reminded me that I'm allowed some comfort, even if it's in the form of food, so I can be a loving mommy and a reasonable wife. I'm so grateful that she—and Sophie and Gina—held me to account not to a momentary and possibly ill-advised goal, but to the larger purposes of my life.

If your friend has sworn off sugar for healthful reasons, it sucks for you to buy her a cupcake. Accountability includes supporting, not undermining, our friends' goals for themselves. But if swearing off sugar is part of an obsession with body image that she is trying to overcome, then an appropriate "calling out" might be, "Get off the treadmill and eat a cupcake already."

Our Issues and the Lies Behind Them

Just as encouragement is never a one-size-fits-all undertaking, accountability is highly specified and requires a compassionate heart toward our friends and a working knowledge of their issues.

After years of friendship and endless hours discussing our issues, I can make a pretty comprehensive list of them, including our flaws, fears, bad habits, and stinking thinking patterns. See if you find any you can relate to:

- Trouble expressing feelings or even knowing how we feel. This leads to *behaviors* like dishonesty, manipulation, and resentment-provoked passive aggression and *feelings* like depression and anxiety.
- Being dishonest about our needs and desires or not even knowing what they really are.
- Fear of failure or disappointment, which keeps us from being able to set goals and stick to them.
- Not setting boundaries with kids, in-laws, bosses, PTA members, and occasionally our husbands.
- Enmeshment with extended families and friends, in which we take on the problems of others as if they are our own, thereby neglecting to manage our own lives.
- Anxiety over money. Among us we are either too frugal and controlled (fear driven) and have trouble spending money on ourselves for things like haircuts and doctor's visits, or we are overspenders who can focus too much on materialism and struggle to live within our means.
- Workaholism. You don't have to even get paid for your work to be a workaholic. We struggle to rest and recreate. See chapter 7, "Sabbatical Sisters." Busyness and social media

addictions are also in this category, because these issues all have to do with our sense of worth and needing constant assurance of it.

- Addictions to food, alcohol, sugar, and caffeine. All addictions in some way are connected to comfort. We're all struggling to find healthy ways to self-soothe and seek connection.
- Perfectionism related to, but not limited to, body image, mothering, work, relationships, housekeeping, following Jesus. Perfectionism is a branch of legalism and leads to shame. It also threatens our identity in Christ and our acceptance of grace.
- Inaccurate expectations of marriage, ranging from too low to unrealistically high. Laziness in our relationships and discontent arc the results. Over the last ten years, I've also had friends whose husbands were unfaithful to them and/or verbally abusive; in every case, these friends have had issues with setting limits on these toxic behaviors.
- Indecision over our life path, fear of making mistakes or taking risks.
- Chronic anxiety over health, money, our kids, our future, relationships with family, whether or not we are getting life right.
- Trouble being on time and/or overcommitting our time (part of the boundaries issue).

As we've explored these issues and their origins over coffee, over the phone, on long walks, in support groups, in prayer, in therapy, and via text, my friends and I have discovered underneath each of these issues some lies that we picked up in our youth and have believed ever since:

- You are a troublemaker.
- You are "too much."

- You are a burden.
- You are responsible for others' (siblings, parents, other family members) feelings and well-being.
- You're a bad daughter, wife, mother, Christian.
- You're not worth protecting.
- You aren't very capable.
- God is going to punish you for your past.
- You don't have what it takes.
- Your faith is too weak.
- If you're going to make it, you're going to have to make it on your own.
- No one understands you.
- You're unlovable.
- You aren't enough.

All of these issues are related to identity. I bet you can relate to some of them and have struggled to silence some of these lies. I also hope, with all my heart, that you have a friend you have talked to about these things. The single most valuable form of authenticity that I share with my best friends is when we speak out loud the untruths that get stuck on repeat in our minds. Saying them out loud helps us refute them.

I'm thickheaded, and occasionally I keep believing some of the above lies. But remember the enemy's wickedness and his motive behind them: to kill, steal, and destroy the abundant life and unique callings that God has for me as a wife, mother, daughter, teacher, writer, and friend. As I fellowship with my friends, they recognize when I'm speaking those lies out loud, and they tell me. They know—as much as human beings *can* know—what God intends for me, and they want his will to be done in my life.

Essentially, this is what all accountability should be about: to help each other believe the truth, that we are dearly loved and made for a purpose—and act like it!

Overcoming Our Issues

When I first met Gina, my Sabbatical Sister from chapter 7, we were both serving on a women's ministry team. We didn't really get to know each other until I was officially acting as her mentor while she served as MOPS coordinator. We ended up with a routine: I would pick up our kids at school on MOPS days, and she would come get them at my house but stay for another hour, telling me about her joys and challenges as a leader. Her challenges almost always fell under the same category. She had great discernment and wisdom, but she struggled to speak her thoughts and feelings out loud; she had trouble expressing authority. Over time, I held her accountable to doing the hard work of leadership: casting vision as well as making some choices that would displease a few people on her team.

I now know that we were chipping away at a much larger issue in her life. A middle child and consummate peacemaker, growing up without the knowledge that God loved her, Gina had always struggled to speak her thoughts and feelings aloud. Though Gina hears Jesus' voice with clarity as much as anyone I know, she still occasionally battles the lie that her job is to do what others think is right, what will keep the peace, which can make following Jesus' instructions difficult. These days, Gina mentors me in life as much as I do her, but I still hold her accountable to speaking up when she needs to; I still remind her that as a child of God, hearing the Holy Spirit is her birthright and she answers to God alone.

In essence, I hold Gina accountable to her identity in Christ. She does the same thing for me. She knows better than anyone that I still struggle to feel valuable if I'm not keeping a punishing speaking schedule. When I've been overbooked and an engagement gets cancelled, it's Gina that I call when I feel like a loser because I have a day off. She reminds me that I don't have to be stressed out to be valuable and that God wants me to have peace and rest. I have also given her the name My Slow-Down Friend. I do *not* struggle to speak up in conflict, but the opposite. When I feel like going into a situation with guns blazing, Gina is the one I call. She will always take a deep breath—which I find infectious. I'll take one too. Then she'll methodically make me unpack my annoyance verging on rage, until I've calmed down and talked myself out of a rash behavior. She's kept me out of several nasty situations and possibly also jail. And in the bigger picture, Gina has helped me to understand why I get so reactive. She prays for me and she helps me heal.

Don't Bury Your Talents or I'll Kill You

Another way friends hold each other accountable to wholeheartedness and identity is pushing each other to use our gifts. I love the movie *Good Will Hunting* and only wish it had 95 percent fewer f-words so I could let my teenage daughter watch it. Far-fetched though the "boy genius from South Boston" premise might be, the screenplay holds some truly beautiful messages about love. Math genius Will (Matt Damon) has the undying loyalty of his friend Chuckie (Ben Affleck), who will get him a job if he can, lie to Will's girlfriend if he's asked to, and beat a guy up just because he used to bully Will in kindergarten. Though Chuckie isn't doing the holiness thing great, he demonstrates the wholehearted accountability piece pretty well. When Will talks about hanging out in South Boston for the rest of his life, living next door to each other and taking their kids to little league together, Chuckie makes the speech at the top of this chapter. (I've edited out all the f-words.) Basically, he says if Will doesn't cash in on his talents and live up to his potential, he'll kill him. He might mean it literally.

Jesus made sure we knew, in no uncertain terms, that he expects us to make good use of our gifts. In the parable of the talents, the servant who buries the money he was meant to invest is called wicked and lazy. I don't want God to call me either.

Sisters, we need someone who will threaten us with bodily harm and harassment when we don't use our talents, because our talents are connected to our callings—the great purposes of our lives. Our good works bring God glory, heal the sick, comfort the weary, free prisoners, raise children, care for the poor, feed the hungry, build bridges in society, make advances in science and medicine, put a stop to racism, overpower darkness, and make an eternal difference. If you believe that the enemy is trying to stop you from using your gifts, you will recognize that you need a support system to succeed. When you create anything—a family, a ministry, a piece of art, a friendship, a new business—you are most like God, the Creator. And Satan hates you. Yes, you, sitting there at your kitchen table or in the cab of your truck or in front of your computer in your cubicle. And you will not beat him alone.

I've had a pretty great year in ministry. I've been able to reach exponentially more women than I have in any year before, I've written both vacation Bible school and junior high curriculum that's been read by hundreds of kids, I've spoken at the largest convention for moms in the world, and I sold my first book (you're reading it). The *day* before each one of these major events came to fruition, I was feeling absolutely crushed by frustration and near despair. In each case I called Jen, Gina, or Josie (sometimes all three) and asked them for prayer. They always prayed like I asked them to, but they also told me I was not allowed to quit. I'm not being melodramatic when I say I literally couldn't have done it without them.

Jen particularly has helped me track the ups and downs of this spiritual warfare and remembered with me the timing of these attacks and the way they were always a sign that God's victory was close at hand. The pattern became so clear that when I called her in discouragement, she knew immediately that something big was about to happen. She has never questioned my competence in ministry, not because she believes I'm awesome (though she kind of does, which is really nice), but because she truly believes that I'm doing what God has called me to do, and so he will equip me. It would be a sin of faith to give up.

Jen's core lie is, "You are not good enough." While my core issue is wanting to be loved, Jen's is wanting to be seen as valuable. Both are crises of identity, and both attack our callings. I can always, in good conscience, turn around and remind Jen of all that she has been called to in her life, all that she has endured and overcome, and what specific skills, talents, and spiritual gifts God has blessed her with. When she's afraid to step out or is in a waiting period for God to give her direction, I can always say with confidence and passion that she *cannot* give up. And I say it with wonder and awe at her character: though she worries about her own value, she never fails to lovingly encourage me in mine.

Defending Our Friends' Freedom

Speaking of the f-word, this week Jen coined a brilliant phrase: the "What the Fudge Were They Thinking Ministry." (Because I know all the scriptures about swearing and coarse language by heart, please make sure that the *F* always stands for *fudge*.) In this,

Jen is paraphrasing the insightful and incredibly funny author and spoken-word poet Amena Brown, whom we heard speak at a convention. One of Amena's friends offers her a "Cuss Word Ministry," the blessing of calling a really bad situation she's in by a really strong name. Amena feels great relief that someone gets the gravity of the situation.

Jen's version is very specific: it's the situation in which a friend is being treated badly but doesn't recognize it. In this case, we say, "WTF was he/she thinking? He/she can't treat you like that!"

Wholehearted accountability includes giving our friends perspective about mistreatment or abuse and a reminder of what they're worth. Sometimes mistreatment has become habitual, or they are too close to the situation to see it clearly. Sometimes they don't see it clearly because their childhood experiences have shaped them to tolerate something intolerable. In still other instances, some of us will put up with a lot of hurts in the name of Jesus, trying to be loving and turn the other cheek as he taught us. Sometimes all these factors come together.

Jesus is a lion as well as a lamb, and he is not in favor of the oppression of his people. Remember how he railed against the Pharisees for giving the Jews a heavy load of ticky-tack rules to follow? Do you recall how he overturned the tables of the money changers in the temple, who were cheating the working-class worshippers as they came to buy their offerings to the Lord? Do you remember how he said those who cause children to sin should tie a rock around their necks and jump in a river? And do you remember how he called Saul/Paul to account, asking him why Paul was persecuting him by persecuting his followers? We can bring the same kind of righteous indignation to bear for our girlfriends, letting them know when we see them moving past being gracious and into being a doormat.

Gina and I were at a women's Bible study at our home church two years ago, and we met a nice young newlywed. She began sharing some of her challenges of new married life, and Gina and I (both married for more than fifteen years) were offering an encouraging and sympathetic ear, assuring her that her trials were normal. But then the young woman said something like, "He's only left bruises on my arms a few times." Gina and I both went white. We looked at each other in dismay, then simultaneously said something like, "No, no, no, no! That's *not* normal! That's *not* okay." The woman looked shocked. I'm very sorry to say that we never saw her again. She did not want to see what we were reflecting back to her. I don't know if we should have handled that differently; but at the moment our hearts were in the right place. We wanted desperately for this bride to know that she could stand against physical abuse in her marriage. She is worth more, made for more. I pray for her still whenever she comes to mind.

I'm so grateful that among women I walk closely with, the WTF Were They Thinking Ministry has met with better results. My girl-friends and I have been recipients of various types of mistreatment throughout the decades: verbal abuse, manipulation through guilt, being lied to habitually, unrealistic demands by employers, even a husband's infidelity. In every case, we have been loved and strengthened by friends who were brave enough to say to us, "This is bad. You're not crazy. You should—and can—put a stop to this."

If our ultimate goal in wholehearted accountability is to help each other live out God's purposes for us, then helping our friends have good boundaries is key. Oppressed, overworked, ill-treated women aren't a good representation of God's heart to the world. Bible verses about being patient and kind were never meant to keep us in abusive situations or allow us to be beaten down and discouraged.

Please, my sisters, prayerfully speak up when your friends are being harmed or pushed past healthy limits. Not all calls for WTF Ministry are acute. If your friend's lie is "You are too much," or "You are too sensitive," even in a healthy marriage she may need support to set healthy boundaries or ask for what she needs from her husband. The young mama whose kids are running her ragged or whose teenagers are talking back more than they should could use a little shot of "Stand Up for Yourself" too.

Ask and You Shall Receive

I'm a big fan of asking. If you're going out to eat, you want me with you, because I will humbly ask for just the kind of table we want (not too near the kitchen or screaming children, warm enough that we won't shiver, but not in direct sun so we'll sweat), and more often than not, we'll get that beautiful table. If the server brings our food out very late or with several errors, I will kindly accept their apology and then sweetly say, "Free dessert?" It almost always works. Hurray! Dark chocolate for everyone, just because I asked!

Wholehearted accountability is dessert, my darlings. "Gracious words are a honeycomb, sweet to the soul and healing to the bones," says Proverbs 16:24. But you might be missing out because your friends are sweet, mild-mannered, and not wanting to call you out without your permission (they either have great boundaries or they are big chickens!). But I believe your friends have these to give you: gracious words that whisper, "You are known. You are valuable. You were made for a purpose. You can do this. I won't let you give up." Ask to hear them. And give them when you're asked.

Chapter 12

THE PRAYER FACTOR

(Maybe Read This Chapter First)

M'Lynn, you're in my prayers.

—OUISER BOUDREAUX IN *STEEL MAGNOLIAS*

When I think about a group of friends with issues, Jesus' disciples are the first who come to mind. Talk about a group of guys who never should have gotten along. They were from different economic backgrounds and tribes, different professions, and among them were both a traitor to Israel (Matthew, the tax collector for Rome) and one who wanted to take Israel back from Rome by force (Simon the Zealot). And yet these men went on to change the world through their mutual faith, love, and encouragement.

So, I like what Peter, after years of Christian service and evangelism, writes about relationships in 1 Peter 4:8: "Above all, love each other deeply, because love covers over a multitude of sins." Or, as *The Message* puts it, "Most of all, love each other as if your life depended on it. Love makes up for practically anything."

After reading the pages of this book, even with all the tips, research, examples, and Scripture I've referenced, with all the formulas and descriptions of "deal-breaker issues," you may still be wrestling with this tension: When do I show grace and when do I speak hard truths? How do I know when to speak and when to listen? How do I find the right words to restore my friends? How do I know when to call them to account in a kind way? How can I tell when I'm being judgmental and when my concerns are justified? The answer will always be the same: love like our Father in heaven loves. And in this, we are all going to fall short sometimes.

But this story about my father on earth helps me:

When I was seven years old, I had an obsessive fear of stinging insects. The front walkway of our home was bordered by flowering shrubs, a hot spot for bees in the spring. My middle brother was fearless, catching the bees in jars with his bare hands, but I was afraid to walk out to the driveway. To make matters worse, there was a huge wasp nest in a tree on my school playground, and I was afraid to go out to recess, a neurotic little second-grader leaning up against the wall as all the other kids ran out to the swings.

My dad tried to talk me out of my fear, but when his reasonable explanation of the habits of wasps didn't alleviate it (the classic, "They won't bother you if you don't bother them" routine), he did something grand. He waited for dark, got a long-handled broom out of the garage, and went to the schoolyard. With reckless disregard for his own well-being, he knocked the wasp nest out of the tree and stomped the wasps to death.

My dad did a heroic thing (and I think my mom probably put him up to it, so she gets love credit in this story as much as he does, though she did not face bodily harm). Dad took away the thing I was afraid of, clearing a path for me. Often when I hear people discuss what love is, I think of my dad knocking those wasps out of the tree.

When we come face to face with our friends' flaws, quirks, and even irrationalities, much of the time our job is to bear them and even clear a safe path for them. I worked in women's ministries for many years, and here's the main lesson I learned as a leader and a shepherd: just because you see someone's blind spot doesn't mean it's your job to point it out. As it says in Ephesians 4:2, "Be completely humble and gentle; be patient, bearing with one another in love."

I believe we are being loving when we use hand sanitizer a little more than is probably necessary around the friend who worries about germs. We show love to our friends who are usually running late by bringing a book while we wait for them (or possibly telling them we need them there thirty minutes before we really do). We let the friend who talks a little too much bend our ear a little longer than we feel like being on the phone. We make an extra effort for the birthday of the friend who needs a little more attention than our other friends do.

These are small, loving sacrifices that make each other feel safe. They say, "You can be who you are, and I will not try to change you to make *my* life more convenient." They are the equivalent of my dad knocking down the wasps' nest. Our friends may eventually become less germophobic and more punctual—just as I got over my fear of stinging insects—but in case they never do, we will bear with their small stuff in order to stay in relationship with them. And as we give others grace, I believe we get better at receiving it.

On the other hand, when I think of my earthly father, the wasp story stands out because my dad was the person who most often told me to be a brave risk-taker. He seemed to believe I could do anything. He pushed me into my first wave on a boogie board long before I thought I could do it, and he was right. I could do it. He made me do other things that scared me, too, like truth telling, or getting up on a stage to sing. He helped me grow up to be braver, kinder, and better than I would have been without his influence.

So it comes to this: love means knowing when to allow our closest friends to stay right where they are, and when to tell them it's time to move past fear, and help them be brave so that they can do all the things they love and be who God is calling them to be.

God certainly loves us like this, only better, because he's the perfect Father: he loves us unconditionally, but he also reveals the truth about us at the right time so we can receive it and be transformed. His love prevents him from crushing or condemning us with the truth, even though he may reprimand us and dole out a consequence. Sometimes he protects us from harm, and other times he allows us to be hurt in order to make us stronger, braver, freer, and closer to him. His purpose is always couched in his love for us, helping us to be more wholehearted for his glory.

I want to be a woman who loves my friends this way, and thereby draws friends like this, without competition or comparison but with a heart for one another's good. Though we are frail, though our flesh is weak, when we cozy up to God's heart we become more like him. We learn to trust in his timing, which gives us the wisdom to speak at the right time, to hold our tongues at the right time, and always, always to pray for God's goodness to be at work in our friends' lives.

Pray for Yourself

Part of me thinks this last chapter should have been the first because this truth is foundational. If you want to be a good friend, get to know your Father.

Everything I've encouraged you to do in this book is nearly impossible without God's help. By nature, humans face an unavoidable paradox: we want to be loved more than anything, but our self-centeredness and sin makes us behave in ways that push people away from us. Our desire to be loved works against us, causing us to be overly needy, insecure, and even manipulative. We all, on some level, hate what Jesus said, that if we cling to our own life we will lose it, but if we give it up, we will keep it. How do we know that this is really true? How do we put ourselves out there and love unselfishly when we are so desperately needy of love ourselves? It's the ultimate jump from the lion's head (another *Indiana Jones* reference, I'm getting old).

I can't rely on my own good intentions and loving character to deliver authenticity, encouragement, accountability, tough love, and truth. Before I began writing this book, as I've shared in earlier chapters, a friendship with a dear friend fell apart and I agonized about the loss on a spiritual level. And then on a completely twelve-year-old-girl level, I actually counted how many women I still had in the "favorites" section of my iPhone; for pride's sake, it just felt bad to have someone drop off my roster.

So, in many ways, I'm still an unsafe person. My friends can be unsafe too. But they continue to become safer and saner through pursuing God. The resource that has most influenced the writing of this book is Cloud and Townsend's *Safe People*. At the end of their book, they write, "The chief theme of the entire Bible is reconciliation of unsafe relationships. . . . This means that no relationship can be let go without a struggle to negotiate and resolve problems."[1] The point of understanding safety in relationships is not to blame others and leave, but rather to learn how to reconcile. And the first relationship we have to reconcile, daily, is the one we have with God.

To live in safe, sane, reconciled relationships, consider the prayer factor as *the* factor.

My first duty in being a praying friend is to pray for myself.

The boldest, scariest prayer is at the top of my list: show me the truth about myself. When I entered twelve-step recovery years ago, inspired by my friend Jen, I wrote this on a card with the below verses and posted it in my laundry room:

> Proverbs 17:10: A sensible person accepts correction, but you can't beat sense into a fool. (CEV)
> Proverbs 11:2: When pride comes, then comes disgrace, but with humility comes wisdom. (NIV)

Warning: don't pray this prayer if you don't want God to answer it, because he really seems to enjoy saying yes to this request. Solomon was rewarded for asking for wisdom, and James says God will give wisdom to any believer who asks without finding fault with them. You might not always enjoy the answers, but it's good, oh so good, to be wise and sensible, rather than a fool in disgrace. My relationships with everyone—not just my girlfriends—have been improved by asking God to give me a clear picture of myself so that I can be humble and wise.

Second on the prayer list is to confess sins. In twelve-step recovery I've learned the concept of keeping a short list of wrongdoings. In step ten, we practice taking a personal moral inventory daily, and when we are wrong, we promptly admit it to both God and the ones we've wronged. A daily inventory and confession almost guarantee improved relations with people.

The third duty in prayer is to ask God to meet my needs. Psalms 37:4 says, "Delight yourself in the LORD, and he will give you the desires of your heart" (ESV). My dad started reciting that verse over me when I was a child, and I chose it for my daughter's life verse when she was dedicated to Jesus in our church as a baby. The verse doesn't mean that if I love God he will give me everything I think

I want, but rather he will give me what I *actually* want: to be loved, comforted, and purposeful. Friendships are a way that God meets my desires, but he meets my need for love first with himself. If I go into my friendships feeling unloved, totally anxious, and insecure, there isn't a girl in the world who's going to be able to love me well enough. (However, he has often used my girlfriends to comfort and love me.)

Fourth, I pray for God to repair and restore my perception of reality, to recalibrate the filter through which I see the world and the people in it (this is a subject for a whole other book).

Pray for Your Friends

After you have thoroughly prayed for yourself, pray for your friends.

I like listening to my friends' issues and giving them help and advice when I can. But I believe that praying for them is what will help them most.

Start with praying steps three and four for your friends: for God to meet their emotional needs for love, connection, and purpose, and for God to calibrate their perception of reality. Lovely side benefits shall be yours when God grants these requests for your friends. First, it gets you off the hook for meeting all their emotional needs. I'm sure you are an awesome person, but you're a really lousy God, and your love will never make them complete like God's can. Trust me. I've tried it. Secondly, if God grants them a wise and discerning eye, they will have a clearer picture of *you*. Since you've asked them to give you feedback, tough love, and accountability for both holiness and wholeheartedness, pray this passionately. You don't want crazy, off-the-wall advice. You want God-calibrated, Spirit-filled input.

Then, pray for your friends' troubles. Don't just text "I'm praying for you." Actually pray for them, with fervor, with Scripture, in Jesus' name. Some of my most precious times with God have been in praying for those I love. I also have rich time in God's Word when I'm interceding for others in prayer. The Holy Spirit illuminates Scripture not only for me but also for them. I'll often send the verses God gives me for a friend in a text or email, and they'll say it was just what they needed. Be gentle in this, though, ladies. If your friend just got in an argument with her sister-in-law, don't send a corrective scripture, like "Those who love to talk will experience the consequences, for the tongue can kill or nourish life." Rather, I send *encouragements* from the Bible, verses I know will help them combat the lies they are trying to overcome in their lives, by reminding them of their identity in Christ and God's faithfulness to them.

Pray for your friends' dreams. If you've followed the instructions in this book or agree with their intentions, then you are seeking to wholeheartedly support the purposes of God in your friends' lives. Pray for God to make those purposes clear, that they would be assured of their calling, that God's favor would multiply their efforts, and that they would partner with God in persistence. Remember Elizabeth back in chapter 5 who blessed Mary for believing God's word to her. Do likewise.

Pray for them to be protected from the enemy. With your restored heart and your recalibrated eyes, you see the enemy's purposes in your friends' lives as well as God's. Bind him through prayer in the name of Jesus.

Pray together. If you are a prayer warrior, you are ready to just bust out in prayer over your cell phone while you're standing in Restoration Hardware looking at discount bedding. (Fifteen minutes ago, my friend Wendy actually did this for me.) But many of you balk at this; it's potentially the most risky, intimate thing I've asked you to do in this book. A lot of us don't have that immediate instinct to pray. We say earnestly, "Please pray for me," and if some-one says, "Ok, let's do it right now," we think, *Really? Right here in Starbucks?*

Yes, right there in Starbucks, hold hands and bow your head. Or keep your eyes open if you want to be more stealth about it. But invite Jesus into this friendship, this problem, this circumstance *right now*. Jesus said, "Where two or three gather in my name, there am I with them" (Matt. 18:20). Anytime we are in authentic con-versation about our lives with other friends who love Jesus, we are on holy ground. But let's unite his *presence* with his *power*, which is available to us in prayer. I love my small-group Bible study, which I have attended Tuesday mornings for three years, and my favorite time is our prayer request time. But we spend more time on sharing prayer requests than praying. I am at least 60 percent responsible for this because I am a long-winded storyteller and haven't yet tamed my tongue in this matter. Perhaps publishing this will hold me accountable. Anyway, I'm aware that our group would likely be more victorious if we spent more time in prayer together. And the same is true in our friendships. You don't have to be in prayer request mode to pray. Just pray.

And finally, thank God for your friends. Paul writes in Philippians 1:3–6, "I thank my God every time I remember you. In all my prayers for all of you, I always pray with joy because of your partnership in the gospel from the first day until now, being confi-dent of this, that he who began a good work in you will carry it on to completion until the day of Christ Jesus." Your girlfriends who know Jesus are not just your friends: they are partners in the gospel with you, bringing a message of reconciliation to the world. Not only do you strengthen each other to do God's work in the world, your friendship itself is God's work in the world. Friends who love each other with a holy affection for one another's well-being are so countercultural and so beautiful to behold that they become a witness to the goodness of God and his power to transform hearts from self-centered and deceptive to loving and honest.

Paul's prayer in Philippians 1:9–11 is my prayer for you:

That your love may abound more and more in knowledge and depth of insight, so that you may be able to discern what is best and may be pure and blameless for the day of Christ, filled with the fruit of righteousness that comes through Jesus Christ—to the glory and praise of God.

Thank God for these women that love you, issues and all. Thank God for the heart he's given you to love them. And then, as Peter says in 1 Peter 4:8, "Love each other as if your life depended on it," because it does.

READER'S GUIDE

In my own quest to face my issues, particularly my codependent tendency to try to carry other people's loads, God led me to Romans 12:18, which says, " . . . as far as it is up to you, do your best to live at peace with everyone." I now rigorously pursue self-awareness so that I can do my part to be authentic and encouraging, to extend grace and be truthful, and to confess when I've failed my friends. I'm sure I still have blind spots, but there's one big lesson I've learned: no matter how well I hold up my end of the relationship, sometimes a friend isn't willing to carry hers. If she isn't, then peace, safety, authenticity, encouragement, and accountability just aren't possible no matter how hard I try. This understanding has brought more peace to my relationships, as I've been able to let go of trying to force a friendship to thrive.

This Reader's Guide is designed for those of you who want to do a little extra work. The questions under "Unearthing Our Issues" are intended to help you with your authentic self-awareness journey. The "Deal-Breaker Issues" are summaries of the warning signals indicating that your friend, at this time, may not be able to do her part. I hope and pray that God will bless your efforts to establish a protective fence of safe friends, that you may live wholeheartedly in community.

Chapter 1

CALLS FROM THE BATHROOM: BUILDING AN AUTHENTIC FOUNDATION

The Main Issue:

As flawed human beings, we have a natural bent to hide our authentic selves through secrecy, image management, or withdrawal. To overcome these obstacles and receive the joyful, healing gifts of knowing people on a deep heart-level, we have to make a sacrifice of time and energy to get to know people in real life, in real time, and not just through social media or over the phone. Getting to know each other through fun outings, serving each other or people in our community, and learning together allows us to reveal ourselves authentically and get to know the character of others. We also need to grow in wisdom about the difference between authenticity and intimacy, learning to trust people with our innermost thoughts and feelings in measured doses after we've made an investment of time.

The Deal-Breaker Issue:

While engaging in real-life, real-time behaviors, issues like dishonesty and chronic anger (especially rage) should be red flags. Though they are forgivable sins like any other, they are also the type of character flaws that will make intimacy difficult, especially when and if you ever get into conflict (see the scripture below).

If a new friend only feels comfortable communicating through text or over the phone and is rarely comfortable talking face-to-face, then that may be a sign she is incapable of intimacy at this time. Give her a chance, though. Some women take a long time to warm up, and social awkwardness is not a fatal flaw. However, if you sense her strong need to control how and when you communicate, that is usually a sign of a deeper issue. Friends like this may be trying to control their interactions because they are hiding an addiction (either theirs or someone's close to them) or an unsafe or abusive relationship (with a spouse or another friend). Pray for them—and recognize that they may not be capable of intimacy at this time.

Unearthing Our Issues:

1. Why do you think so many women in our culture are feeling lonely today?
2. Do you have friends who have been in your life for many years? In what stage of life did you meet? Why do you think those friendships have stood the test of time?
3. Which suggestions for making friends and growing relationships most appeals to you? Why?
4. How do you feel about having people in your home? What is the story that your home tells about you? Why might you feel insecure about inviting people in?
5. When you spend time with a new friend and see a potential red flag about her character, what do you do?

Scripture:

Proverbs 22:24–25: Do not make friends with a hot-tempered person, do not associate with one easily angered, or you may learn their ways and get yourself ensnared.

Chapter 2

NUTS AND GIFTS: AUTHENTICITY AND SELF-AWARENESS

The Main Issue:

If we want to be a safe friend and thereby make friends with safe people, self-awareness is key. Being willing to share authentically what we know about ourselves is also critical. Add to this a willingness to examine the underlying source of our issues, and we have the potential for remarkable relationships. You don't have to share your big issues on your first three get-togethers. Instead cultivate a willingness to ask questions, listen carefully, and cover one another's sins with love.

The Deal-Breaker Issue:

If a friend can't acknowledge that she has an issue and remains in a defensive, prideful, or dishonest posture as the friendship pro-gresses over the course of several months or years, accept that deep intimacy isn't possible at this time. I'm not talking about sunglasses placement or parking preferences, but larger issues of character such as honesty, self-awareness, wisdom, and the ability to admit hurtful behaviors. Not being able to acknowledge imperfections is more damaging to relationships than the imperfection itself, and you should take it as the warning sign that it is.

Unearthing Our Issues:

1. Are there any common issues that you share with your best friends? What "mutual craziness" helps you relate to one another?
2. How do you feel when someone shares their issues with you?
3. How comfortable are you letting people know about your struggles, fears, or character flaws?

4. What character quality in a friend makes you feel safe? What quality makes you feel unsafe?
5. Think of a situation that makes you hysterical. Can you point to an event in your life or a past relationship that gives you insight into that feeling? Could you share that new awareness with a close friend?

Scriptures:

- 1 Peter 4:8: Above all, love each other deeply, because love covers over a multitude of sins.
- James 5:16: Therefore confess your sins to each other and pray for each other so that you may be healed.
- Romans 12:9: Love must be sincere.

Chapter 3

PERFECTION IS FOR YO-YOS: FINDING WISDOM AMONG IMPERFECT WOMEN

The Main Issue:

Perfectionism is the enemy of risk-taking and authentic relationships. We have to go into new friendships with the expectation that we are dealing with flawed people, including ourselves. But we should also pick friends who we enjoy being around; friendship shouldn't feel like an endurance test. When discerning the difference between wise, safe friends and foolish, unsafe friends, use the scriptures as your guide.

The Deal-Breaker Issue:

The Bible defines fools as those who are reactive, angry, proud, impulsive, and unwilling to own their issues In the foolish, these aren't momentary lapses in judgment or self-control but character deficiencies that pervade their lives. Don't enter into close relationships with women who habitually exhibit these behaviors.

Unearthing Our Issues:

1. Describe the qualities of your idea of a perfect friend. Do you have one friend who possesses these qualities, or have you found these attributes in different women?

2. What are some of your qualities that make you a fun, safe friend?

3. What are some of your flaws that could sometimes make you tough to get along with?

4. Do you think you struggle with perfectionism in relationships? Do you tend to dismiss people too easily? Or do you let them get away with too much?

5. Have you ever been friends with or are you currently friends with a woman who demonstrates foolish attributes? If so, how is that friendship working out? How do you feel after spending time with her? How could spending a little less time around her positively affect your life and spiritual growth?

6. Do you recognize any foolish traits in yourself? Take a little time to write them out and invite God to set about correcting these behaviors and attitudes in you.

Chapter 4

I'M SO SENSITIVE: HURT FEELINGS AND AUTHENTIC APOLOGIES

The Main Issue:

Handling hurt feelings and conflict in a direct way is essential for authentic friendships. We need to be brave enough to tell our friends when they have hurt, angered, or disappointed us so that they have the opportunity to make it right and so that we don't allow resentment to build up in our hearts. Also essential is the practice of making sincere apologies—owning our harmful or hurtful behavior without defensiveness and justification. This satisfies our innate desire for justice and allows us to keep our relationships free from resentment and bitterness.

On both sides, give grace and allow each other time. Practice the one-week rule. Bring up grievances within a few days, in private, and allow a few days for someone to be able to own her part.

The Deal-Breaker Issue:

"Fools mock at making amends for sin," says Proverbs 14:9. A woman who won't offer a sincere apology or repent of a hurtful, habitual behavior should not be allowed on the inside of your life. Conversely, a friend who persists in resentment and unforgiveness when you have sincerely owned up to wrongdoing is unsafe as well.

Unearthing Our Issues:

1. Which is more difficult for you: admitting you are wrong or telling someone you think they have wronged you?
2. Why is it hard to admit you are wrong without justifying, blaming, or making excuses?
3. Who in your life is a good model of making humble apologies?
4. How do you know when you can truly overlook a friend's offense and not resent her in the long run? Why is it important to sometimes do that, and not bring up every hurt feeling or slight?
5. How do you feel when someone apologizes to you? Does that inspire you to apologize to others?

Chapter 5

IN LIEU OF FLOWERS, PLEASE SEND EMOJIS: DAILY ENCOURAGEMENT IN ITS MANY FORMS

The Main Issue:

There's no such thing as one-size-fits-all encouragement. Ephesians 4:29 tells us to "build others up according to their needs." This type of healthy encouragement comes from authentically knowing our friends' goals, values, strengths, and weaknesses.

The most meaningful way to encourage our friends is in the direction God wants them to go and the opposite of the direction that Satan wants them to go. The first step to this empowering practice is to really listen so that we can know who these women are and what God is accomplishing in their life. Make it a priority to develop friendships with women who share your desire both to spur one another on to love and good deeds, and to pray for each other and for the Lord's timing in your lives.

The Deal-Breaker Issue:

Many people offer encouragement in the form of unsolicited advice. Though they mean to help, you may find yourself routinely feeling hurt, diminished, or guilt-ridden by their instructions. Because many of us are unaware of our motivations in being quick to advise others, the problem can often be solved by simply saying to the advice-giver, "I appreciate how much you care about me, but I'm not asking for advice right now." Mature women can listen and support you without feeling the need to fix your problem.

Unearthing Our Issues:

1. As a busy mom, I'm a texting encourager. But my mother-in-law tells me of a Bible study leader in the 1970s who encouraged her to have a birthday card ministry, making sure to always send friends cards on their birthdays. What is your favorite way to encourage others?
2. What is your favorite way to receive encouragement?
3. Think of a struggle you are currently undergoing. Do you have a friend who knows about it? How could she encourage you?
4. Scripture is a great way to encourage our friends, which is one of my favorite reasons to be in the Word regularly. Have you ever been reading the Bible and felt the stirring to send a scripture to a friend? Did you follow it?
5. Who was the last person you asked for encouragement? Why did you need it?

Chapter 6

SABBATICAL SISTERS AND SELF-CARE: ENCOURAGING OUR BESTIES TO TAKE A BREAK

The Main Issue:

We all need encouragement toward self-care because the enemy is so deeply committed to keeping us exhausted and in bondage to guilt and unworthiness. We need to infuse with courage the women in our life who begin to say no to excessive busyness, even when that busyness is in Jesus' name, reminding each other that Jesus commands us to rest, take a sabbath, and rely on him.

The Deal-Breaker Issue:

If you struggle with the bondage of busyness and have serious trouble giving yourself a break, beware the friend who adds to your to-do list without regard to your well-being. Henry Cloud says that those who love us, love our no as well as our yes. If you have a friend who is consistently making unreasonable demands or doesn't respect your need to have limits, bring that friendship before the Lord and consider if it's one in which you can continue.

Unearthing Our Issues:

1. Do you struggle with taking time to rest and rejuvenate? What keeps you from enjoying sabbath rest?
2. Who can you count on to encourage you in self-care?
3. Have you ever been the friend who doesn't respect someone else's no and/or asks her to serve and show up beyond her comfort level? How can you repent of this and better respect her need for downtime in the future?

Chapter 7

TWO SUPERHEROES AND NO SIDEKICK: OVERCOMING COMPETITION, COMPARISON, AND CODEPENDENCY

The Main Issue:

Competition damages friendships, but even comparison can make us sick. While culture pits women against each other, followers of Jesus should seek to be mutual encouragers. Our friendships should be a safe place not only to be broken, but also to be strong, and to share our strength with others. In Christ, we all have equal value, though our strengths are different. Offer loving encouragement when you see a friend using her gifts and talents to the glory of God.

The Deal-Breaker Issue:

A friend that is consistently competitive is an unsafe friend. Watch for sneaky signs of competition: not only how she might belittle your accomplishments or sneeze on your joy, but how she might put herself down in comparison to you, a subtle, manipulative bid for you to build her up or tear yourself down. Don't jump through those hoops.

Also, beware of the friend who is trying to make you her project. Let her know that though you may have issues, you want to be seen as someone who brings gifts to the relationship as well.

Unearthing Our Issues:

1. Have you ever had an archnemesis? What made you want to judge or compete with her?
2. Who can you count on to be a co-superhero in your life?
3. What are the character qualities, spiritual gifts, or possessions that you are tempted to envy? Has that envy ever hurt a friendship that could have been mutually beneficial?
4. What are the areas in which women in your life compete most?
5. Do you ever make bids for your friends to build you up or tear themselves down, such as "Oh, you're such a good cook. I'm hopeless in the kitchen"? How can you give compliments and encouragement free of that competitive undertone?
6. Can you relate to any aspects of "the fixer disease" or codependency? Ask God to show you that he wants to love and heal you, not just send you out to love and heal others.

Chapter 8

FUNERALS, BIRTHDAYS, AND BABY SHOWERS: ENCOURAGEMENT IN JOY AND GRIEF

The Main Issue:

Encouragement can be expressed in important events and rituals, whether they are celebrations or occasions that mark grief. Romans 12:15 says, "Rejoice with those who rejoice; mourn with those who mourn." Don't miss the opportunities to encourage your friends in their uniqueness or in moments that matter to them. Don't rush them out of their grief. Be courageous enough to sit with them in sorrow, and let Jesus fulfill his promise to comfort those who mourn.

The Deal-Breaker Issue:

Not all our friends have to be able to handle our messy pain, only those we hold closest to our hearts. I have a rule of thumb: if a friend is the one I would want in my living room after tragedy strikes, then I better be in hers when she is brought low.

Unearthing Our Issues:

1. What is your favorite way to offer encouragement to others?
2. What is your favorite way to receive encouragement? When was a time that someone did this for you?
3. Who in your life needs encouragement to continue to just be their fabulous selves? Make a plan to show her love in this way.
4. Who in your life is in need of encouragement in sorrow?
5. Is it difficult for you to spend time with someone who is grieving? Why or why not?
6. Who in your life would you trust to come sit *shiva* with you?

Chapter 9

TELL ME THE TRUTH: ADVENTURES IN ACCOUNTABILITY

The Main Issue:

Accountability between treasured friends who follow Jesus is designed by God to be a mutual source of encouragement, comfort, and restoration. Be wise and love those who rebuke you. Also, be loving and wisely rebuke those you love, according to the Scriptures, using these steps: rebuke, comfort, and attempt to restore. Accountability is a dangerous adventure that may cause temporary conflict, but just as Jesus rebukes and disciplines those he loves (Rev. 3:19), we can love and be loved through holding one another to God's beautiful, life-giving standard.

The Deal-Breaker Issue:

When you attempt to restore gently a friend who is caught in a clearly biblically defined sin and she won't receive the correction, it's okay to get some physical and/or emotional distance from the relationship, hopefully just for a season. Though it's a painful truth, the Bible tells us not to be "teamed up" closely with those who are living foolishly.

Unearthing Our Issues:

1. Whom have you invited into your life to hold you accountable to the teachings of Christ?
2. If a friend were to "call you out" in a sin, what approach would you be most likely to hear? What words and timing would make you feel the least defensive?
3. Describe a time that someone has called you to account. What was the result?

4. Have you ever rebuked someone and been hated for it? What was the long-term result?

5. Have you ever felt hurt by a rebuke that came from someone who was not close enough to walk out the restoration with you?

6. Have you ever rebuked someone "willy-nilly" who was not yours to rebuke? How can you repent of this in the future?

7. Why do you think the issue of accountability is so confusing in the church?

Chapter 10

THE YEAR EVERYONE GOT A BOOB JOB: ACCOUNTABILITY IN THE FACE OF INDIVIDUALITY

The Main Issue:

Accountability is not about making someone more like you or imposing a goal on them which you have set for yourself. Such behaviors are usually rooted in (1) selfishness—commonality makes for simpler communion—or (2) insecurity—the fear that only one of you can be right. Embrace the scriptural truth that each follower of Christ has a different calling, measure of faith, and freedom. They hear the Holy Spirit their own way about their own issues. Treasure the diversity of conviction among your friends as a gift that challenges and sharpens you in your own walk with Jesus.

The Deal-Breaker Issue:

If a friend needs you to see things her way, or doesn't respect your yes and no, try lovingly approaching her and telling her what you are experiencing. She might not be aware that she is coming across as domineering (don't use that word when you speak to her), and your honesty may help her grow in confidence that it's okay for you to be close even if you don't agree on all things.

Unearthing Our Issues:

1. Talk about a few personal convictions that you and your friends hold in common.
2. What is a standard you hold for yourself that some close friends don't share?
3. How diverse is your group of friends on topics such as child-rearing, money, diet, and politics?
4. How comfortable are you when your Christian friends make different choices than you do?
5. How does it make you feel when someone tries to convince you to adopt one of their convictions or lifestyle practices?
6. Have you ever adopted someone else's conviction or practice after watching their example? Have you ever seen a friend follow your example?

Chapter 11

GET OFF THE TREADMILL AND EAT A CUPCAKE ALREADY: ACCOUNTABILITY TO WHOLEHEARTEDNESS

The Main Issue:

Wholehearted accountability focuses on helping each other live out our identity in Christ, in order that we might glorify God. Share your God-given dreams and goals with one another and ask for specific encouragement and "checking in" when you need it. As we encourage one another in practical goal setting and achievement, we also remind each other of our inherent worth because of God's love and grace. With a working knowledge of our friends' issues, we can help them recognize when Satan attacks their value and undermines their purpose. We also stand with one another in setting good boundaries and pursuing other healthy relationships.

The Deal-Breaker Issue:

Sometimes, when we speak up that we see our friends being mistreated, they might not be ready to hear it or see it. Some women will walk away from you once you see the true nature of the difficult situation they are in: whether it is an abusive romantic relationship or another friendship in which they are being manipulated. Therefore, exercise prayerful caution before you exercise the What the Fudge Were They Thinking Ministry. Read on to the final chapter, about how prayer better equips us to be the kind of friends our friends most need.

Unearthing Our Issues:

1. Let's do what you've been wanting to do from the beginning: name some of your friends' issues. But not their names.
2. What are some of the lies about worthiness and identity that you see your friends believe?
3. What is the core lie of your life? What does the enemy whisper to you in your most challenging moments? Does anyone close to you know what this lie is?
4. Name a God-given dream for your life. Who can you trust to share this dream for you and hold you accountable to pursuing it?
5. Have you ever been a recipient of the WTF Were They Thinking Ministry? How is having an outside perspective helpful when you need to set good boundaries?
6. How can you encourage a friend toward wholehearted living this week?

Chapter 12

THE PRAYER FACTOR: (MAYBE READ THIS CHAPTER FIRST)

The Main Issue:

If we truly desire healthy, loving relationships, we should seek the ultimate source of love and wisdom in prayer. Receiving the love of God helps us enter more securely into friendships. Praying for ourselves, specifically for self-awareness and discernment, equips us to offer encouragement and accountability to our closest friends. Then, pray for those you asked to speak truth into your life so that they will be equipped to do so.

Unearthing Your Issues:

1. Who in your life can you count on to pray for you?
2. In reading this book, how has God revealed some areas in your life that could use healing? Can you commit to bringing these issues to him in prayer?
3. Who in your life is in need of prayer right now?
4. How can praying for your friend help you keep a healthy perspective about your friendship with that person?
5. How can praying for your friends' issues help you with the desire to "make them" change or take your advice?
6. And finally, a challenge: when you see evidence of jealousy, competition, or codependency crop up in your friendships, pray for God to heal those issues in you and to guide your friends.

ACKNOWLEDGMENTS

Thank you to my agent Keely Boeving and WordServe Literary for taking a chance on an unknown kid. Your edits, insight, and ability to talk me down from trees has been invaluable. Jenny Baumgartner, intrepid editor extraordinaire: your vision birthed this book and your unbridled enthusiasm kept me going until the end. Someone should sew you a Marvel-style costume. Maybe me? And to Brigitta Nortker and the rest of my team at Thomas Nelson: you have been so good to me. Thank you to David Stoop and Jack West for making essential connections and giving me encouragement. Thank you to MOPS International for all you do to raise women leaders, and what you have given me personally. Elisa, I got on the right bus at the right time, and you were God's gift to me. Vivian, without your suggestions TN would never have found me. Our Starbucks dates have been pivotal moments in my life.

To Terry: you warned me at the beginning that you would let me down. But you never have. Your marshmallow fluff love and mitten-covered punches to the throat have always come at the right time and in the right order. Jennifer: your Enneagram 9 bad-assery couched in empathy was just what I needed. To my brothers in recovery: Ira, Sam, and David, thank you.

To all the friends who let me share their stories, thank you for your courage (and, in many cases, thank you also to your husbands). Josie, honey bee, shopping partner, editor, debater of all things, most clever of all texters, funny, wise, winsome, and servant of God. Some of the best lines in this book are yours. Twenty-one years we've been together. Thank you. Gina, dreamer, prophetess, prayer warrior, and my soft place to land. You accept all my weirdness and celebrate it. Thank you. Jenni, superhero, teacher, champion, cheerleader. We will be friends when we're eighty, and maybe living in our seaside cottage by then. You wrote this with me, along with the story of my life. Thank you. Jana, you were there in the depths. Let the mutual mentoring continue. Thank you. Jodi, you're great on paper but even better in person. Thank you for your loyalty and love. (Eric, love you, too, brother.) Jenny and Jill, I'm blessed and lucky to have you in my tribe and on my street. May our dorm-like adventures never end. Pom, photographer and tech support, thank you for all the help you've given me at one-twentieth its market value. Sophie, God gave me you at the right time for all the right reasons! You've taught me about how to succeed. And all the others: Wendy P, Kelly, Elizabeth, Laura, Wendy H, Barb Eun, Yuka, Jayme, Michele, Karen, Carmella, Becca, Melissa, Audrey, and all my CODA sisters. You've saved me so much money on therapy. Okay, the orchestra is playing me off stage.

To Mom and Dad: thank you for always believing that I could do this, and just about anything else I wanted to try.

Sophia, you are the Rory to my Lorelai, but with better boundaries and a happy ending. May wisdom be your constant guide, my beloved firstborn. Olivia, you are my sunshine, my fiercest cuddler, my comic relief. May peace and faith be not just your name but your constant attendants, my creative "baby" daughter.

Jeff, my partner, my financial backer, my friend, my rock for twenty years and counting, and my best accountability partner: after all, you're my Wonderwall.

NOTES

INTRODUCTION

1. C. S. Lewis, *The Four Loves* (New York: HarperCollins, 1960), 90.

CHAPTER 1: CALLS FROM THE BATHROOM

1. David Zailer, founder of Operation Integrity, "Step Five: Sharing Your Inventory," November 11, 2018, Mariners Church, Irvine, CA.
2. Jill Hubbard, *The Secrets Women Keep: What Women Hide and the Truth That Brings Them Freedom* (Nashville: Thomas Nelson, 2008), 83.
3. Kira Asatryan, "How Texting Can Strengthen a Relationship," *Psychology Today*, February 11, 2015, https://www.psychologytoday.com/us/blog/the-art-closeness/201502/how-texting-can-strengthen-relationship.
4. Cortney S. Warren, "How Honest Are People on Social Media?" *Psychology Today*, July 30, 2018, https://www.psychologytoday.com/us/blog/naked-truth/201807/how-honest-are-people-social-media.
5. Hubbard, *Secrets Women Keep*, 14.

CHAPTER 2: NUTS AND GIFTS

1. Henry Cloud and John Townsend, *Safe People: How to Find Relationships That Are Good for You and Avoid Those That Aren't* (Grand Rapids, MI: Zondervan, 1995).
2. Milan Yerkovich and Kay Yerkovich, *How We Love: Discover Your*

Love Style, Enhance Your Marriage (Colorado Springs, CO: Waterbook Press, 2006).

3. Yerkovich and Yerkovich, *How We Love*, 33.

CHAPTER 3: PERFECTION IS FOR YO-YOS

1. Don Hamachek quoted in Patricia Schuler, *Voices of Perfectionism: Perfectionistic Gifted Adolescents in a Rural Middle School* (Storrs, CT: University of Connecticut, 1999), 6.

2. Anne Lamott, *Bird by Bird: Some Instructions on Writing and Life* (New York: Anchor, 1995), 28.

3. *Julie and Julia*, directed by Nora Ephron, written by Nora Ephron and Julie Powell (Culver City, CA: Columbia Pictures, 2009), DVD.

4. "Why Did Jesus Warn Against Saying the Word *Raca* in Matthew 5:22?" Got Questions, https://www.gotquestions.org/raca.html.

CHAPTER 4: I'M SO SENSITIVE

1. Beth Moore, "Session 5: Peace Be with You," 62:00, MP4, from *Living Beyond Yourself: Exploring the Fruit of the Spirit* (Nashville: LifeWay Press, 2004).

2. Peter Scazzero, *Emotionally Healthy Spirituality: It's Impossible to Be Spiritually Mature While Remaining Emotionally Immature* (Grand Rapids, MI: Zondervan, 2017), 31–32.

3. Scazzero, *Emotionally Healthy Spirituality*, 44.

4. *The 12 Steps and 12 Traditions Workbook of Codependents Anonymous* can be found on the CoDA Resource Publishing website: https://www.corepublications.org/product/twelve-steps-twelve -traditions-workbook.

5. Harriet Lerner, "The Power of Apologizing," *Psychotherapy Networker*, March/April 2018, https://www.psychotherapy networker.org/magazine/article/1150/the-power-of-apologizing.

CHAPTER 5: IN LIEU OF FLOWERS, PLEASE SEND EMOJIS

1. "Parakaleo," from *Thayer's Greek Lexicon*, found at Bible Tools, https://www.bibletools.org/index.cfm/fuseaction/Lexicon.show/ID /G3870/parakaleo.htm.

CHAPTER 7: TWO SUPERHEROES AND NO SIDEKICK

1. Dr. Henry Cloud and Dr. John Townsend, *Boundaries Updated and Expanded Edition: When to Say Yes, How to Say No to Take Control of Your Life* (Grand Rapids, MI: Zondervan, 2017), 99–100.
2. Cloud and Townsend, *Safe People*, 29.

CHAPTER 8: FUNERALS, BIRTHDAYS, AND BABY SHOWERS

1. Gary Chapman, *The Five Love Languages: The Secret to Love That Lasts* (Chicago: Northfield, 2015).
2. C. S. Lewis, *A Grief Observed* (New York: HarperCollins, 1996), 3.
3. Dacher Keltner and Paul Ekman, "The Science of 'Inside Out,'" *The New York Times*, July 3, 2015, https://www.nytimes.com/2015/07/05/opinion/sunday/the-science-of-inside-out.html.

CHAPTER 9: TELL ME THE TRUTH

1. *When Harry Met Sally*, written by Nora Ephron (Culver City, CA: Columbia Pictures, 1989).

CHAPTER 11: GET OFF THE TREADMILL AND EAT A CUPCAKE ALREADY

1. Brené Brown, *Daring Greatly* (New York: Penguin Random House, 2012), 10.

CHAPTER 12: THE PRAYER FACTOR

1. Cloud and Townsend, *Safe People*, 189.

ABOUT THE AUTHOR

Amanda Anderson likes to believe that the *Friends* theme song was written for her and her girlfriends. A woman without sisters, she prizes her friends—ages twenty-eight to seventy-two—for their wisdom, sense of adventure, knowledge of their own issues, and unconditional love.

Amanda is a Bible teacher, speaker, blogger, and freelance journalist in Orange County, California. Her speaking ministry, Heart in Training, reaches young mothers, women's ministries, and 12-step recovery groups around the country. Having overcome a decade-long struggle with anxiety and depression, her message now focuses on learning to follow our good God and actually enjoy it: through resting, play, creating healthy boundaries, risking authentic relationships, and releasing perfectionism. When not writing or speaking, she is sewing quilts at her kitchen table, talking on the phone with her girlfriends, hunting for vintage treasures with her husband of twenty years, or embarrassing her two daughters by dancing in public.

To inquire about booking Amanda for a speaking engagement, contact her through her website www.heartintraining.com.